Holy Superheroes!

Exploring the Sacred in Comics, Graphic Novels, and Film

REVISED AND EXPANDED EDITION

Greg Garrett

Westminster John Knox Press
LOUISVILLE • LONDON

Holy Superheroes! Exploring Faith and Spirituality in Comic Books was originally published in 2005 by NavPress.

Unless otherwise identified, Scripture quotations are from *The Message* (MSG). Copyright © 1993, 1994, 1995, 1996, 2000, 2001, 2002. Used by permission of NavPress Publishing Group. Other Bible versions used include the King James Version (KJV) and the New Revised Standard Version (NRSV).

Scripture quotations from the New Revised Standard Version of the Bible are copyright © 1989 by the Division of Christian Education of the National Council of the Churches of Christ in the U.S.A. and used by permission.

Book design by Drew Stevens
Cover design by Jennifer K. Cox
Cover illustration: Images.com/Corbis

Revised edition
Published by Westminster John Knox Press
Louisville, Kentucky

This book is printed on acid-free paper that meets the American National Standards Institute Z39.48 standard. ∞

08 09 10 11 12 13 14 15 16 17 — 10 9 8 7 6 5 4 3 2 1

Library of Congress Cataloging-in-Publication Data

Garrett, Greg.
    Holy superheroes! : exploring the sacred in comics, graphic novels, and film / by Greg Garrett. — Rev. and expanded ed.
        p. cm.
    ISBN 978-0-664-23191-0 (alk. paper)
    1. Comic books, strips, etc.—Religious aspects.   2. Comic books, strips, etc.—United States.   3. Comic books, strips, etc.—Moral and ethical aspects—United States.   4. Motion pictures—Religious aspects.   5. Motion pictures—United States.   6. Motion pictures—Moral and ethical aspects—United States.   I. Title.
PN6712.G37   2008
741.5'3382—dc22   2007039282

Holy Superheroes!

Also by Greg Garrett

The Gospel according to Hollywood (2007)

For Chris,
who puts on the cape every morning

Contents

Preface

You may have picked up this book because you're a comics fan who wants to learn more about the religious, mythic, and cultural elements of your favorite stories. You may be reading because you're taken by the characters who have become a part of our culture and who fill the screens of our TVs and multiplexes week after week: Spider-Man, the X-Men, the Justice League, the Fantastic Four, Daredevil, Superman, Batman, Neo and Morpheus, Blade, the Hulk, Hellboy. Or you may be someone reading as a person of faith who wants to know whether this most American of art forms really does say anything useful about spirit, salvation, how we're supposed to make our way in this world.

All of you are welcome here, and all of you should find something to your liking, because all of you are reflected in my own feelings and questions about American comics and their many incarnations. I'm going to say a few words about how this book will work and the material we'll cover, and then I'll get out of the way and let you satisfy your curiosity.

First, the approach: this book isn't a historical study of comics, a superficial fan frolic, or a purely aesthetic study of the art form; there are already other books that can do that for you with some facility. Likewise, it isn't a scholarly tome you'd need to be Lex Luthor or Dr. Strange to decipher. Instead, this is a book written for an intelligent general audience and built around what's called "philosophical reading," which means that we'll be studying comics for wisdom on how to live our lives. Along the way, we'll engage religion and theology, American culture and history, the interrelationships between comic books and other art forms, and the current superhero mania in

American culture, but my primary interest is in understanding what comics have to tell us about issues that are of lasting importance: justice, violence, faith, patriotism, peace, power, belief, damnation, and redemption.

Since the most influential faith tradition in America is Christianity (and it's also my tradition), I'll be referencing largely Judeo-Christian ideas, but I'll be bringing in other faith traditions, thinkers, and philosophers when it seems appropriate. In some places, we'll be following the old Christian tradition of studying "exemplary lives," examining characters who can teach us things about how we might live, something like the old genre called "saints' lives," stories of Christian saints and martyrs that were circulated to teach and inspire people in the days before Superman, Batman, and the Fantastic Four. The saints' lives themselves are really early stories of superheroes: through their faith, the saints often performed superhuman physical and spiritual feats, bona fide miracles.

I think that with comics we're also dealing with some powerful myths, stories that express a truth somehow beyond rational meaning. In the modern age, we got used to the idea that rational thought and empirical data were the only ways to solve a problem, to find the truth. Now, it seems we're coming back to an understanding that by downgrading myth, we lost an important element from our lives. In earlier days, as theologian Karen Armstrong points out in her book *The Battle for God: A History of Fundamentalism*, myth was regarded as a primary way of understanding the world, "concerned with what was thought to be timeless and constant in our existence. . . . [It] looked back to the origins of life, to the foundations of culture, and to the deepest levels of the human mind. Myth was not concerned with practical matters, but with meaning."[1]

We've gotten into the bad habit of thinking of myth as something false, or, at best, something untrue—like those Greek gods and snake-headed monsters—rather than something that is supremely true; we've made the mistake of thinking that myth is untrue because it can't be proven, rather than something supremely true because it's a story that has to be accepted. Faith and belief are at the heart of mythic questions, and I'm suggesting that the long popularity of the heroes and stories we're going to discuss in this book rises from the way they've filled a mythic gap for us in a world that has become more secular and more rational. We read about, watch, care about these stories because we need them; I've long believed that the stories that move us are the ones we most need to hear to be whole. So, in some crazy way, these stories filled with violence and people in leotards draw us closer to the sacred, inspire us in our own quest to do good. And the "how" of that is the subject of this book.

As for the subject matter of this book: while I'll be referencing a range of comics published in the past sixty years, most of them will be contemporary series with a substantial readership, or filmed versions of comics that are familiar to millions of people. Most will come from the two publishers who dominate the field, DC and Marvel, or their imprints. Most will be "superhero" comics, since those are the most pervasive and most popular stories for Americans, and the ones that most seem to call for a mythic understanding.

So while I may mention a few lesser-known comics with powerful faith and life lessons, mostly you'll be reading about characters you'll readily recognize. And although I like some of them and they're now widely read in America, I won't be dealing with such things as Japanese manga, because those stories are not a mythic reflection of our culture and don't feature our particular take on issues of faith and justice. Since most of you reading these words are Americans, I'm assuming you will be most interested in understanding the powerful American myths expressed in these stories of superheroes.

Finally, a little about me, so you can know what biases, interests, and expertise I might claim. First, although you'll see that I've learned a lot from different faith traditions and respect them greatly, after seeking answers in a lot of places, I returned to Christianity because of a set of life experiences I've written about elsewhere. I've completed three years of full-time seminary education, and my final answer to many of life's questions comes from my faith. You'll find many of my conclusions in the pages that follow, although no one person speaks for the entire Christian faith. Experience suggests that some Christians will agree with what I say here; others will think I don't go far enough in one direction or another, don't reference the Bible enough, or shouldn't even be trying to reconcile faith and culture. Whatever you believe (or don't believe), I hope this book will stimulate your thinking—and will encourage you to exercise your faith.

As to expertise, I'm a fiction writer (several novels and a lot of short stories), professor (I teach film, fiction, and American literature at Baylor University, and classes on writing and theology at the Episcopal Seminary of the Southwest), and popular theologian (author or coauthor of books on *The Matrix* films and on film and theology and of a number of articles and essays on popular culture, spirituality, and story). So I'm writing this book from my standpoint as a storyteller and student of popular culture.

But I'm also writing as a longtime fan, since I started collecting comics so many decades ago I'm afraid to even say. These days, it's true that I read Henry David Thoreau and Thomas Aquinas, Martin Luther King Jr. and Thomas Merton, the Dalai Lama and Paul Tillich. I read books on politics, ecology, history, and theology. I read novels by Margaret Atwood and essays by Anne Lamott.

But I also read *Astonishing X-Men* and *Powers, Justice League of America* and *Daredevil, Hellblazer* and *New Avengers, Captain America* and *Fables, Ex Machina* and *Planetary.*

I've read comics all these years because they represent some of the best storytelling around. I read them still because I've grown to love many of the characters. But I've also kept reading because I find something powerful and useful between these glossy covers: wisdom on how to live my life.

I hope this book will spotlight some of that wisdom for you now.

Greg Garrett
Austin, Texas
May 2007

Acknowledgments

I'm grateful to my family, particularly my sons, Jake and Chandler, for tolerating and encouraging me in this enterprise. Jake, especially, read, talked about, and followed along with what I was doing. My mom and dad handed out the allowance that let me start reading comics many years ago, and my brother Jeff was my cohort in collection back then. Jeff went from being a boy with a closet full of superhero comics to being a Southern Baptist pastor, further proof that there's something to this whole religion and comics thing. And I could not be more proud.

Thanks to David Dobson, who wanted to bring this book over to Westminster John Knox, America's best publisher of works on religion and popular culture. It's a joy to work with him and all the wonderful professionals at WJK.

Thanks to the Austin Public Libraries, particularly the good folks who work at the John Henry Faulk Library downtown. I performed most of the research that led to these pages in the company of the homeless men and women who come to the library to get out of the weather or catch up on their reading. Their presence was a constant and welcome reminder to me of the need for justice in the real world as I thought about theology and wrote about characters in leotards.

Thanks to Baylor University for the 2003 summer sabbatical that freed me to do some of the initial research and writing for this book, and thanks also to Baylor provosts David Lyle Jeffrey and Randall O'Brien for their support of my writing and of serious consideration about faith and culture. And as ever, I'm indebted to my students at Baylor, who keep me ever thinking and learning.

Thanks to my rector and friend Greg Rickel, and to the parishioners of St. James' Episcopal Church in Austin, Texas, for their affection and support of my writing, seminary training, and vocation. St. James has been a force for peace and justice since its beginnings; may it continue to do that good work with courage and energy in the years to come.

Thanks to my friends Hunt Priest and Roger Joslin, both fine writers and thinkers, who talked theology and culture with me in the spring of 2004 as I finished the initial draft of this book. Thanks to Martha Salazar, who didn't cringe when I said things like "I have to go to the comics store," and who walked alongside me during the revision of this book.

Finally, special thanks to my buddy Chris Seay, who suggested this book because he believed that the culture and I had something worthwhile to say on some important subjects. Admiring someone you love is one of the great joys of this life; so is being able to work with that person on projects that engage your mind and stir your soul. My life has been filled with such joys. That's why this book is dedicated to Chris, and why I'm proud to claim him as my dear friend.

Introduction

Comics and Religion

"Look, up in the sky!"

A few years ago something earthshaking happened in one of my favorite comic books. Now this is nothing new in *Fantastic Four*, one of the oldest and most popular Marvel Comics series; its heroes regularly confront cosmic villains who threaten to transform our beautiful green planet into something resembling a hunk of burned toast. What I'm referring to, though, is something quiet—and at the same time, one of the most moving things I'd ever read in a comic book.

In this story, a character known as "The Thing"—a test pilot named Ben Grimm, who back in 1961 (in our time) was changed by cosmic rays into a superpowerful sentient pile of orange rocks—stands over an injured old man in his old neighborhood, and is sick at heart that with all his power there is nothing he can do for him.

Then he realizes: "No . . . No, there is one thing."

And then, Ben Grimm, idol of millions, one of the most powerful of superheroes, drops to his knees and begins praying in Hebrew: "*Sh'ma yisrael adonai! Eloheinu adonat echad . . .* Uhm . . . *baruch shem k'vod malchuto l'olam va'ed.*" A comic book superhero, davening.[1]

1

The Thing was, after thousands of appearances, revealed to readers as a person of faith. Well. And it only took forty years to tell us. But there was more than just this one poignant revelation. The old man, Mr. Sheckerberg, revived, actually engages Grimm in a discussion about faith: "All these years in the news, they never mention you're Jewish. I thought maybe you were ashamed of it a little?"

To which Grimm, standing in shadows, but with a street-light over his head bearing witness to his illumination, replies, "Nah . . . anyone on the Internet can figure it out, if they want. It's just . . . I don't talk it up is all. Figure there's enough trouble in the world without people thinkin' Jews are all monsters like me."

In reply, Sheckerberg reminds Ben Grimm of the Jewish legend of the Golem: "He was a being made of clay—but he wasn't a monster. He was a protector." *Like you*, is his point, and perhaps further, he means to say that in some ways Ben Grimm too is a servant of the Holy.[2]

So, let's review: A character from a popular culture narrative drops to his knees in a tough situation. Touching, I'm sure. A character reaffirms his religious identity. OK. But the Golem, for crying out loud? The Golem was an inanimate man-shaped lump of clay that served as the legendary protector of European Jews in the Middle Ages. He would come to life only when a *ba'al shem*, a holy rabbi who knew the secret names of God, used a sacred formula to breathe spirit into him.[3]

I think we can agree that this intimate knowledge of a faith tradition is more than mere surface trappings, way past a simple acknowledgment that some sort of supreme being may exist somewhere or that prayer may be the only answer to a situation. And this we find in a funny book?

But as Jeffrey Weiss pointed out in an article on the comic for the *Dallas Morning News*, this sort of thing is "a small indication of a shift in the way our culture deals with faith."[4] As people of faith become more comfortable creating art—and as artists of all sorts become more comfortable including spiritual elements in film, music, and comics—such references are bound to show up. And this trend makes comic books—where good and evil, right and wrong, justice, mercy, and the power of love have long been important themes—a terrific place to look for revelation.

A terrific place—and an increasingly influential place.

When I first wrote these words in early 2004, we had just passed the end of what *Christianity Today* film critic Jeffrey Overstreet was calling "the year of the comic book hero."[5] *Daredevil*, starring Ben Affleck; *The Hulk*, directed by Ang Lee; and *X-Men II* had all been released in 2003. So was *The League of Extraordinary Gentlemen*, drawn from the erudite comic by comics scribe Alan Moore. *The Matrix: Reloaded*, written by former comics writers the Wachowski brothers, became the most popular R-rated film of all time, and along with its sequel, *The Matrix: Revolutions*, the anime films collected in *The Animatrix*, and the popular video game *Enter the Matrix*, created a cottage industry that made headlines and magazine covers across the country. *Road to Perdition*, adapted from the graphic novel by Max Allan Collins, and *From Hell*, drawn from the graphic written by Alan Moore, premiered—and, since then, so did *Spider-Man II* and *III*, *X-Men III*, *Batman Begins*, and *Superman Returns,* among many others. As I write, the box office surprise of 2007 is *300*, the gritty action film adapted from Frank Miller's graphic novel of the same name, a movie that sold over $300 million in tickets worldwide in its first month and prompted *Business Week* to point out its lessons for the rest of the film industry.[6] Looking at the movies, TV series, and video games still in the pipeline, it would probably be safe to say that this year—and next year, and the year after that—will also be the year of the superhero. Screenwriter, producer, director—and former comics writer—David Goyer affirms, "Comic books are hip now. Every studio has at least 10 projects in development based on comic books. A lot of filmmakers are comic book fans—Sam Raimi and Guillermo del Toro and Bryan Singer. They've made it socially acceptable in Hollywood."[7]

Perhaps the most significant sign of how pervasive comics have become, however, comes from how far they've filtered from the comics shops and multiplexes into mainstream culture. A few years ago in the pages of *Entertainment Weekly*'s highly anticipated "Power" issue, Hollywood's most powerful actors, producers, and directors were rendered as comic book heroes: Julia Roberts as Wonder Woman, Bono as the X-Man called Banshee, Adam Sandler as the Riddler. On the cover of the British news journal *The Economist*, a story on the growing economic power of the European Union was illustrated by a caped superhero wearing a jaunty beret—a jarring sight to those who think of the superhero as a strictly American property, and meant to dramatically demonstrate the startling shift of economic might from the United States to Europe. A 2002 cover from the German newsmagazine *Der Spiegel* depicted President George W. Bush and his closest advisors as Rambo, Batman, the Terminator, Conan the Barbarian, and Xena, Warrior Princess. It seems clear that comics and their underlying myths and stories have become a part of mainstream culture—and intimately connected to America.

Pulitzer Prize–winning novelist Michael Chabon won his award in 2001 for the comic-related novel *The Adventures of Kavalier and Clay*, released his own comic book series based on the heroes described in *Kavalier and Clay*, and coscripted *Spider-Man 2*. According to Chabon, "There does seem to be an increased visibility, and perhaps . . . even an increased degree of respect given to comic books."[8] Museums and libraries are collecting them; scholars are presenting papers on comics at academic conferences and writing books about them for academic presses; and after decades of considering them a menace to society, now teachers and librarians are using comics to teach reading, art, and writing. Graphic novels sections are now among the most popular sections of libraries—and among the most profitable sections of bookstores. Interestingly, in recent years, books on religion and graphic novels have been among the few growth areas in publishing.

Of course, that interest in comic characters is nothing new: a dozen of the 250 top-grossing films in history have had comic book roots, and many others near the top—including the *Star Wars* films and the *Matrix* films, share comics sensibilities. Superman, Batman, Spider-Man, even the Teenage Mutant Ninja Turtles, have been featured not only in films but in cartoons and newspaper comic strips, in plays and television shows, in video games and on beach towels, on underwear and fruit roll-ups and lunch boxes and PEZ dispensers, and of course, in their own print comic books and graphic novels.

They represent some of the most pervasive popular culture archetypes ever created, instantly recognizable around the world. Denny O'Neill, longtime writer and editor at DC Comics, home of such mythic characters as Superman, Batman, and Wonder Woman, describes how the best-known characters, like Batman and Robin

> are part of our folklore. Even though only a tiny fraction of the population reads the comics, everyone knows about them the way everybody knows about Paul Bunyan, Abe Lincoln . . . everybody in the country knows about them. They have some of the effect on people that mythology used to and if you get into that you can't avoid the question of religion.[9]

Of course, that's exactly what I'm arguing in this book, that at the very least, comic heroes have become a part of our mythology. In fact, scholars John Shelton Lewis and Robert Jewett have demonstrated in their book *The Myth of the American Superhero* how the stories of Superman and others fit into the narrative pattern they call the "American monomyth":

> A community in a harmonious paradise is threatened by evil; normal institutions fail to contend with this threat; a selfless superhero emerges to renounce temptations and carry out the redemptive task; aided by fate, his decisive victory restores the community to its paradisiacal condition; the superhero then recedes into obscurity.[10]

This description contains words that can't help but radiate meaning to people of faith: paradise, evil, temptation, redemption. We also can't help but notice that the monomyth could be the plot formula for way too many comics over the years: When evil rears its ugly head, Superman (Batman, Flash, Captain America, etc.) steps into a phone booth (Batcave, etc.) to don his uniform and take on his heroic identity; he bravely battles the villainous forces, ending the threat, restoring the state of peaceful equilibrium. Then he vanishes into civilian guise (Clark Kent) and the ordinary world of men and women until the next job for Superman.

With the coming of Superman in 1938, Batman in 1939, and a horde of other masked marvels shortly thereafter, the world discovered a type of storytelling that was both universal and uniquely American, born from newspaper comic strips, from the pulp adventure stories of Tarzan and Doc Savage, and from adventure comics. Comics became a rite of passage, a part of American childhood, and the characters from comics entered virtually every form of popular culture: movies, television, radio, and advertising.

In the 1950s, comics took a tumble. The formula grew tired, some in American society began to consider them lowbrow, and controversy made them seem perhaps even a bit deviant. But in the early 1960s, at the beginning of the so-called Silver Age of Comics, new characters like Marvel Comics's Spider-Man and the Hulk demonstrated a new psychological realism, and comics regained a sense of relevance. Marvel pioneered comics that had continuity—that is, the events of one issue led to and had an impact on events in the next, like life—and Marvel and DC alike began to tackle more topical real-world justice issues like racism and drug abuse.

In the mid-1980s, masterful reinventions of heroism like Frank Miller's seminal revision of Batman in *The Dark Knight Returns* and Alan Moore's and Dave Gibbons's look at heroism in contemporary society, *Watchmen*, made it clear that the old ways weren't good enough. As always, popular culture heroism had to be changed to keep it relevant. Comics became more complicated and more ambiguous in their treatment of themes like justice, violence, and good and evil. This has complicated their relation to the American monomyth, although it looks as though the idea of powerful characters bringing justice to a world that desperately needs it may never go out of style. Even though the terrorist attacks of 9/11 have caused much soul searching in the world of popular culture about the depiction of violence, the role of violence, and the importance of tolerance, the American response to the attacks could have come directly from the American monomyth, as the world's lone superhero suited up for action and launched itself into the blue to violently punish evildoers—and discovered the strengths and limitations of a response built solely around returning violence for violence.

Even as comics grow beyond the simple outlines of a formula, they continue to reflect our fears, desires, and beliefs. While superhero titles still dominate, comics and graphic novels have branched out. They represent today virtually every genre in popular culture storytelling, including crime, horror, fantasy, comedy, science fiction, and romance. They also address real-life concerns, as in the Pulitzer Prize–winning graphic novel *Maus*, which Art Spiegelman wrote and drew about his family's history in the Holocaust; *King*, Ho Che Anderson's multivolume biography of Dr. Martin Luther King Jr.; and Craig Thompson's semiautobiographical *Blankets: An Illustrated Novel*, a poignant and troubling book about a conservative Christian boy's coming of age.

In the process of telling their stories of human—and superhuman—characters, comics deal with issues near and dear to our hearts: faith, hope, belief, guilt, justice, redemption, ultimate meaning, ultimate evil. John Shelton Lawrence and Robert Jewett argue that the American monomyth is actually an ongoing retelling of the Judeo-Christian story of redemption,

> combining elements of the selfless hero who gives his life for others and the zealous crusader who destroys evil. The supersaviors in pop culture function as replacements for the Christ figure. . . . Their superhuman abilities reflect a hope for divine, redemptive powers.[11]

And so they do. We can find in Superman a powerful messiah figure, in Batman an avatar of God's justice. We learn with

Spider-Man that with great power comes great responsibility, with the X-Men that violence is not the solution to bigotry and hatred. We may be inspired by the idea that a supernatural servant of God like the Spectre might actually exist, or be challenged by the faith struggles of devout Christians like Matt Murdock (Daredevil) or Nightcrawler of the X-Men. But whether we read because we need to see good conquer evil or we read as people drawn to issues of faith and spirituality, clearly comics have much to show us. In this book, we'll take them seriously—as seriously as we ought to take every kind of storytelling.

As with all stories, there are things in comics that can change our lives, recognitions that can charge our consciences, and darkness that can sear our souls. We can learn about peace and about its sad absence. We can learn about justice and mercy. We can see great faith and the reality of its failure. We can step into the shoes of those making ethical decisions, decisions we ourselves might face, or have faced.

And if we read wisely, we can discern much about the human condition—and about the world to come.

So follow on, gentle reader. Up, up, and—

Well, you know.

Modern Heroes

Here he comes to save the day.
—Theme from *Mighty Mouse*

People on this rotating globe differ wildly from clime to clime, society to society. Humans have created masculine warrior cultures and nurturing female-dominated cultures, seafaring societies and farming communities; humans are hunter-gatherers and philosophers. But no matter how different the cultures, humans have always needed heroes, real or created, to model behavior, to give hope. *Spider-Man* director Sam Raimi felt the weight of this responsibility:

> Any story of a hero, shows us the good that we are capable of—the value of these types of tales. I knew . . . that millions of kids would come see this movie, I just knew it, and they would look up to *Spider-Man*. . . . Therefore I felt it was very important that I put a morally responsible character up there. Someone that would be worthy of that admiration. . . . Someone who went from somewhat selfish to someone who used their abilities to help others. It's more than beating up the bad guys.[1]

The work of comparative anthropologist Joseph Campbell sheds further light on the shape and power of our hero worship.

In his studies of world religions, formation myths, and hero stories, Campbell discovered that not only do almost all cultures have hero myths, but that, as we will see, they work in surprisingly similar ways both structurally and culturally. Campbell explained it this way: "There is but one archetypal mythic hero whose life has been replicated in many lands by many, many people."[2] In this chapter, we'll talk about the genesis of our heroes, examine the archetypal hero myth to see what it can teach us, and discover what comics teach us about heroism—and how it has changed—over the years.

Comics superheroes have a massive family tree that spreads its branches wide throughout Western culture and history. If you're wondering how characters in long underwear and capes became our archetypal heroes, the answer is that they represent a sort of culmination to centuries of storytelling, history, and heroism. Our American superheroes are equal parts demigods from Greek myth, strongmen and prophets from the Judeo-Christian tradition, literary lions and characters from folktales, and pop culture traditions. Here are some of the more obvious branches.

Western culture takes much of its formative thought from the ancient Greeks, and the *Iliad* and the *Odyssey* of Homer, filled with martial heroes, warring gods, and supernatural menaces, were standard reading for educated people until a few decades back. Other tales we now broadly consider "Greek mythology" contain all the elements of Homer, as well as a stirring cosmology, stories about why the universe is as it is, and other heroic tales: Jason and the Argonauts, Hercules, Daedalus, and the Minotaur. Roman retellings and new tales like Virgil's *Aeneid* added to the literature of heroism, as did tales from Celtic, Nordic, and other cultures.

The Jewish and Christian traditions added their own characters, stories, and symbols, which are known to most educated people in Western culture. In the Hebrew Bible, characters like Moses and Aaron, Joshua and David, wield courage and supernatural power to protect and serve their people. My favorite of the Hebrew characters when I was young, Samson, needs only some long underwear to make his way into the pages of modern comics—any man who could slay huge numbers of foes with the jawbone of an ass, burst ropes by expanding his chest, and push apart pillars to collapse a temple on his enemies is pretty close to prototypical superhero status already. The Hebrew Bible also contains prophets who perform miracles, witches and sorcerers and soothsayers, and warriors and philosophers, some of the greatest characters in any literature.

They were joined by equally compelling characters in the Christian era. There was Jesus, of course, the Messiah/savior whose function lots of comics heroes emulate; biblical scholar Burton Mack argues that the Jesus depicted in the Gospel of Mark, a wonder-working savior who travels from town to town, is the model for the heroes of American popular culture.[3] There were the apostles, who wielded supernatural might, had visions, and often died for their beliefs. There were the saints of the church, all of whom had to have performed at least one documented miracle, and some of whom, like St. Patrick, who rid Ireland of its snakes, St. George, who slew a dragon, or St. Joan of Arc, who led a nation into battle, were bona fide heroes.

To these figures, we could add warriors like Richard the Lion-Hearted, Charlemagne, and Henry V, and contemporary heroes like World War I's Sergeant York and World War II's Audie Murphy. We could include culture heroes of art and thought: Leonardo da Vinci, Michelangelo, Thomas Edison, Albert Einstein.

Finally—and perhaps most importantly, we should include the heroes of legend, myth, and story that permeated the Western world: King Arthur and his Knights of the Round Table, Robin Hood, the Golem, the Scarlet Pimpernel, the Count of Monte Cristo, the Three Musketeers, Deerslayer/Hawkeye, Sherlock Holmes, Professor Von Helsing and the fearless vampire hunters of Bram Stoker's *Dracula*, Tarzan, John Carter of Mars, the Invisible Man, Zorro, and the pulp fiction heroes of the 1920s and 1930s like Doc Savage and the Shadow.

The most important comics creations—archetypal characters like Superman, Batman, Spider-Man, the Hulk, the X-Men—represent the culmination of these traditions, a popular culture marriage of myths and legends and history that has made superheroes the most important mythical messengers of America in the past century. Their stories have permeated every element of our popular culture, and few people aren't at least familiar with the most popular stories, even if they themselves have never picked up a comic.

What superheroes have in common with all of these characters—and what makes them, too, powerful archetypal characters—is their adherence to what Joseph Campbell called the archetypal hero myth, a hero's journey followed by almost every culture hero from Homer's time to ours. The details and structure of the journey may vary slightly, but as we will see, one of the reasons characters like Batman, Superman, and Spider-Man have had such amazing appeal is that they seem to tap into this cross-cultural model for mythic storytelling, which seems to be hardwired into our systems. How else to explain the three-thousand-year reign of a certain story model across almost every known culture? For whatever reason, the archetypal hero story (which is distinct from the American monomyth we talked about in the introduction, although as you'll see, it contains some of the same structural elements) makes a kind of ultimate sense for us.

It was clear to Joseph Campbell through his wide-ranging studies that most of the hero myths that matter concern a culture hero—someone who fights to save or preserve a particular culture, often through his return to that culture with some saving knowledge, power, or wisdom. This is a potent point about heroism: you can't be a hero in a vacuum. Power alone doesn't make a hero; service and sacrifice does, as we'll see in more detail in the chapter on power. As Campbell told Bill Moyers, "A hero is someone who has given his or her life to something bigger than oneself."[4]

The basic shape of the archetypal hero story is simple. It begins with the character in the *ordinary world*, everyday life. The character is then presented with some challenge, a *call to adventure*, a call that is sometimes refused. After finally accepting that call to heroism, the character must cross a *threshold* between the ordinary world and the world of adventure, after which, through trials, adventures, and the intervention of enemies and allies, he or she must muster courage to approach the inner sanctum of the enemy and undergo an *ordeal* that leads to a boon or reward of some sort. The hero then brings the reward back to society, but not without first facing an ultimate test of worth, which sometimes brings figurative or even literal death to the character before a sort of *resurrection* occurs.

This shape should be familiar in lots of ways, first because it parallels the lives of many great men and women. The stories of Moses and the apostle Paul, the Gautama Buddha and Martin Luther King Jr., even the life, death, and resurrection of Jesus conform to this powerful mythical story pattern.

Its shape is also familiar from the most potent modern form of storytelling, movies. In fact, story analyst and script consultant Christopher Vogler has written a valuable book called *The Writer's Journey* demonstrating how the hero's journey shapes most successful movies—and suggesting how contemporary writers can consciously use the hero's journey model to shape their stories. From *The Wizard of Oz* to *The Lion King* to *The Matrix*, movie heroes have followed the same journey as Homer's Odysseus, and comic heroes too walk in these footsteps.

Before Superman became Superman, he was a boy named Clark Kent, an orphan taken in by the Kent family in Kansas. While he had a history that would shape who he was (in dramatic terms, the events of a character's life before the story begins are called, logically enough, "backstory"), at the beginning of the Superman story we are in the ordinary world of a Kansas farm, and Clark Kent was a good, smart, middle-American boy. The ordinary world in the Batman story is that of young Bruce Wayne, the son of wealthy parents, who lived in a mansion outside Gotham City. The ordinary world of the Spider-Man story begins in the Queens neighborhood where Peter Parker, a teenage bookworm, lives with his elderly aunt and uncle, goes to school, takes abuse from jocks, and aspires to be a scientist. The ordinary world for most of the characters who later become X-Men is some sort of childhood, whether in America, Russia, or elsewhere in the world, where however difficult the circumstances, life each day is still life as usual for most people.

The day comes, though—as it comes to all of us—when we are presented with a call to adventure, an initiation, a movement to a different stage of life. For Superman and the characters of the X-Men, the call to adventure comes with the realization that they are different, that they have powers that set them apart from their friends, their peers, their parents. For Batman and Spider-Man, the call to adventure is a tragic one, coming in the form of the murder of Bruce Wayne's parents before his eyes and Peter Parker's refusal to stop the thug who later kills his Uncle Ben. But in all of these cases, the call means that life can never be the same, even if for some of these characters it takes a few knocks for the lesson to sink in.

Before the adventure begins, a threshold has to be crossed, an initiation mastered, some symbolic mastery achieved, and in most of these cases, an outward change reflects the inward changes: a costume. For Superman, Batman, and the X-Men, the costume represents their willingness to be a different person, to assume a heroic role. (Peter Parker had already created a costume as Spider-Man, but he does not assume his heroic role, cross the threshold, until after he captures his Uncle Ben's murderer; until then, he has worn his costume, assumed his role, only to gratify himself.) The costume sets these heroes apart as their powers have set them apart, and with the costume comes a new name and identity. When Superman (or Batman or Spider-Man) is in costume, muscles rippling, he becomes a person very different from his human alter ego, Clark Kent (or Bruce Wayne or Peter Parker).

Often this threshold crossing is managed by a guardian, who can be a mentor figure such as Clark Kent's parents, an ally such as Edna Mode in *The Incredibles*, or a villain such as Spider-Man's nemesis, the Green Goblin. In the recent *Ultimate Spider-Man* relaunch and the first *Spider-Man* movie, the Goblin represents Peter's first great test as a hero. He doesn't yet know how to fight or how to use his powers to their fullest extent, even if he has the courage to stand against a foe as menacing as the Goblin.

Once the threshold has been crossed, however, the adventure is well and truly joined. There is no going back. In this stage of the hero's journey, he or she gains allies in the battle for good, as well as a range of enemies. Batman gains allies like Commissioner Gordon, Robin, and Batgirl to aid in his ongoing quest to rid Gotham City of evil, but he also gains a set of enemies like the Joker, Two-Face, and the Penguin, who stand in the way of that quest.

The world of adventure is where we find most comics heroes, in a sort of extended stasis. Because of the episodic nature of comics, there is no end in sight for most of them, and the characters are currently convening a monthly meeting of allies and enemies as they struggle to bring the world back into balance. Because of the ongoing narrative most comics heroes are involved in, we can more easily see the last stages of the hero's journey in film versions of comics-flavored stories or in graphic novels than in comics series.

In the course of the battles in the world of adventure, the hero encounters an ultimate evil that must be overcome and a boon that must be rescued. The boon may be an elixir, a magic formula, a secret weapon, an antidote, a set of codes or words, or new discoveries that can save the world. But before that happens, the hero must vanquish that evil in the ordeal, which is often a descent into the underworld. In Frank Miller's *The Dark Knight Returns*, the ordeal is a battle between Batman and the leader of the Mutants; in *The Matrix*, written and directed by comics writers the Wachowski brothers, Neo (Keanu Reeves) must enter the stronghold of his enemies to rescue Morpheus (Laurence Fishburne).

Once the reward has been grasped, the hero embarks on the *trip back*, but often there is one more climactic moment, one final test of the hero's tenacity and gifts that brings him to the edge of death and sometimes beyond. In *Dark Knight*, Batman literally dies in final combat with Superman; through his genius with chemicals, Batman has concocted a chemical that will stop his heart and keep him in suspended animation until after the funeral, at which time he is reborn to occupy the caves beneath the Batcave.

In M. Night Shyamalan's *Unbreakable*, the origin story of a superhero, the moment is David Dunn's near-drowning in a swimming pool; as he sinks, tangled in the black shroud of the pool covering, his resurrection comes through the aid of the children he is rescuing from the killer who has come into their home and held them captive. In *The Matrix*, Neo is killed—literally, physically—before being brought back to life by a kiss from Trinity (Carrie-Anne Moss), the breath of life, the power of story. After the final resurrection, these characters are free to return to the society they left at the beginning of their adventures with the knowledge of who they are, what they want, and what their powers are.

In a typical comics issue or story arc, we might see elements of only the last two-thirds of the hero's journey; in a graphic novel or film, we are more likely to see the entire circular process play out. But in any case, their conformity to the elements of the archetypal hero's journey accounts for much of the narrative allure of comics stories, and as we'll see in succeeding chapters, their use of other archetypes and symbols continues to keep them powerful and relevant even today as the world changes and our stories adapt to match. As Sam Raimi put it, one of the reasons *Spider-Man* was so successful was that it used twenty-first–century storytelling: "Like any legend or myth, it has to be retold in a modern way [so] that the audience of the day can relate to it. I think that keeps it vital and fresh and really relatable."[5] All those hero myths that have lasted—those whose stories touch something fundamental in us—have lasted largely because they have found new ways to tell us an old, old story.

Look, Up in the Sky!

Superman, savior of the helpless and oppressed . . . battles the forces of evil and injustice.

—*Action Comics*, August 1939

Long years ago, far from this mortal coil, a wise and powerful father made a fateful decision: to send his only son to a backward planet. There, he was raised by an earthly mother and father, exhibiting signs of the supernatural power he commanded as his birthright, until, finally, he reached adulthood and embarked on his mission: the salvation of the people of Earth. Then he stepped forward, performing miracles that made it clear that he was someone special. Someone godlike.

The year when this savior began his ministry was not, incidentally, circa CE 25. It was, rather, the year 1938.

And the savior's name was not Jesus.

It was Kal-El.

You probably know him better as "Superman."

When two Jewish teenagers, Joe Shuster and Jerry Siegel, created Superman, a superpowered hero who could oppose the forces of evil and who stood for truth, justice, and the American way, the two boys were repackaging a powerful archetype, one who has captured our attention and our interest for over sixty years. Comics writer Mark Millar writes that "Superman resonates with everyone because he's an amalgamation of the legends we've loved for 5,000 years. He's Moses, Hercules, Icarus, and Jesus Christ all rolled up inside one American flag. He's the greatest fictional character of our time."[1]

When Siegel and Shuster created Superman, they changed the face of American popular culture. Although there had been plenty of heroes in comics and pulp fiction, they were all flesh and blood, with fast fists or ready guns, but no advantages over the villains. Now, for the first time, a hero had the power to take on a fallen world, a world where evil loomed and injustice walked. Writer and cartoonist Jules Feiffer has said of the pre-Superman comics that the heroes not only weren't as interesting as the villains, they were no match for them; just a simple look around would show anybody that nice guys finished last. "Villains," he said, "by their simple appointment to the role were miles ahead. It was not to be believed that any ordinary human could combat them. More was required. Someone with a call."[2]

It was easy to see why Siegel and Shuster were led to create a superhuman hero. It was the late 1930s; America was still stuck in the Great Depression. Overseas, Hitler had begun his march of expansion, the Japanese were rattling their swords, and disturbing stories were coming back from the Jews of Europe about the virulent anti-Semitism they were encountering and their growing dread about the future.

In times of trouble, Jews, like all people, have remembered reassuring stories. The first such story was about the Golem, the mythical creation we talked about in the introduction that could be summoned to protect the Jews during the persecutions of the Middle Ages. Comics great Will Eisner has said that "the Golem was very much the precursor of the superhero, in that in every society there's a need for mythological characters, wish fulfillment. And the wish fulfillment in the Jewish case of the hero would be someone who could protect us." And Eisner, like Pulitzer Prize–winning novelist Michael Chabon, believes that Superman is very much the Golem in tights, a direct descendant of this strain of Jewish tradition: "[Jews needed] a hero who could protect us against an almost invincible force. . . . So [Siegel and Shuster] created an invincible hero."[3]

How invincible? Well, the other strain of Jewish thought which finds its way into Superman is also clear: at the heart of things, he is nothing less than a representation of the Messiah, the Chosen One of God: Emanu-El, "God with Us." Let's look first at the given name these Jewish teenagers gave their redeemer, Kal-El. "El" is a word often used in renderings of the names of God in the Hebrew Bible; in Hebrew, "Kal-El" translates to "All that is God." That's some big shoes to fill.

There are other obvious borrowings from Jewish history and situations in Superman's creation and origin: Kal-El is a refugee, one of the few survivors of the diaspora from his planet, Krypton; his salvation as a baby in a spaceship is immediately reminiscent of Moses, who floated in a similar life raft on the River Nile; he comes to a foreign land, where he must reconcile the tension between his desire to fit in—become like the natives he resembles—and the clear evidence that inside, there are things that make him different, alien. It's strange to think of Superman as a Jewish superhero, but unlike many of the Aryan All-American heroes who followed—consider Marvel's Captain America/Steve Rogers, for example—he clearly drew on the shared wishes, fears, and hopes of his creators, and those beginnings were a part of the continuing mythos.

In his early days, Superman was not the all-powerful godlike creation he became; his powers, while amazing, were more modest. In the early days, he really could only leap tall buildings, not fly, and while he was resistant to bullets and superhumanly strong, it's meaningful that the cover of *Action Comics*, which introduced him to America, made only modest claims for his powers. On it, he has raised a car full of criminals over his head, but he appears to be using both hands and all his strength to do so. Compared to his later levels of power, this Superman is eminently human.

It's important to remember that in his early days—in keeping, perhaps, with the Jewish tradition and the concerns of his creators—Superman was just as likely to fight for social justice as legal justice. For every bank robber he corralled, he put away a slumlord. In keeping with the Jewish belief exemplified throughout the Hebrew Bible and in many of the teachings of Jesus, justice is about taking care of the poor and needy, the widow and orphan.

But teenage boys, then as now, were less interested in helping hands than in fisticuffs, and like those fans of the original *Matrix* film who thought there was too much talk and not enough kung fu in *Matrix: Reloaded*, I'm sure Superman's creators also felt the pressure to conform to the popular story lines of the day, those wanderings of the American monomyth that we first examined in the introduction: a villain hatches a plot, the hero steps forward, defeats it, and restores equilibrium. Before long, Superman had developed additional powers—flight, heat vision, freezing breath, and more—and your average slumlord, grifter, or crooked industrialist couldn't keep up. Superman needed supervillains if he was going to remain interesting, and the level of threat went from neighborhood to cosmic.

This hero, in the process of becoming a cultural icon featured in movies, television, toys, lunchboxes, radio, newspaper strips, and just about everywhere else you looked, went from being a simple fighter for justice to a godlike embodiment of the American way, and it's not surprising to note that in this process, control of the character slipped from the hands of the two men who had created him to the corporation that published him. In the course of the next fifty years, as other writers and artists—many of them Gentiles instead of Jews—depicted Superman, it's not surprising that the early Jewish references to the Golem and the Messiah were replaced by more particularly Christian references. I'm sure Mark Millar does not lightly compare a comic book hero to Jesus Christ—but, as we'll see, he's hardly the first person to make the comparison.

Such progression and change is not unusual in comic characters, who are often different versions of themselves based on the interests and stories of the people who write them. (A good example from comics: Kevin Smith's devoutly Catholic Daredevil is very different from Brian Michael Bendis's more morally complex Daredevil, although their depictions are separated by only a couple of years.) And since one of Superman's obvious predecessors is the Jewish tradition of Messiah, it makes perfect sense that he would also reflect images of Jesus, since Christians see Jesus as the fulfillment of those legends.

As the beginning of this chapter suggested, it isn't difficult to find immediate parallels between the life of Jesus as we know it from the Gospels and the origin of Superman. Like Jesus, Superman doesn't fully take on his identity until he is an adult, although some indication of his power and path appears early on. And in the most important story line in the history of the Superman character—and in the history of comics, perhaps, to judge from the way the story was covered by mainstream media—in the early 1990s, Superman was killed in saving the world against a threat called Doomsday, and, after a time, and some confusion surrounding various characters who themselves claimed to be Superman, came back to life.

A possible future death and resurrection for Superman is featured in the Alan Moore–penned *Superman: Whatever Happened to the Man of Tomorrow*, in which Moore consciously echoes the Gospel stories of Easter morning to tell a story of mysterious rebirth: "When Superwoman and Captain Marvel ripped the vault open, it was empty. . . . He was gone."[4] And in the blockbuster 2006 film *Superman Returns*, director Brian Singer goes to great pains (as *Time*'s Richard Corliss notes) to depict "Earth's savior: Jesus Christ Superman."[5] In *Superman Returns*, Superman undergoes a passion almost worthy of Mel Gibson. He is beaten and brutalized, stabbed in the side as Jesus was, dies, and at last comes back to life, even leaving behind an empty tomb of sorts.

Lots of comic book villains come back to life—the Red Skull, Captain America's longtime nemesis, is representative of the policy that no good villain can stay dead long—but the physical resurrection of comic heroes (as opposed to symbolic death and resurrection) is extremely rare, and the conscious decision by the editors and writers of the various Superman titles to create the "Death of Superman" story line and coordinate it among their various magazines is noteworthy. If Superman was already an obvious Christ figure, then this important arc of the hero's journey made him even more immediately comparable to Jesus, as has Brian Singer's version of the death and resurrection of Superman.

We face obvious problems in an attempt to make a one-for-one correspondence of Clark Kent and Jesus of Nazareth, and it's important to point out that popular culture stories use our myths and faith stories as part of a storytelling process, tapping into archetypal figures and deeply held beliefs. But they are *not* those figures or beliefs, and any simple-minded attempt to say "Superman is Jesus" or suggest a depth of coordinated theological truth in any popular culture narrative will usually lead us to grief. Mainstream comic books were not written to be Torah, Sunday school, or madrassah lessons. Our purpose in this book—as it should be in any attempt to study popular narratives to see what they can teach us about life, I think—is to notice correspondences to spiritual and mythological stories, to consider how those correspondences can inspire and instruct us, and not to get too tied up in the ideas that don't fit our purposes. In our book on the spiritual meanings of the *Matrix* films, Chris Seay and I wrote about the character of Trinity in a way that should be instructive to us here:

> As elsewhere in the Matrix films, we should never push comparisons so far that they lose their value. Trinity can simultaneously be *ruah* [the Hebrew word for the Spirit of God], and Wisdom, and Holy Spirit, and the female love interest, and one wicked kung fu babe. One reading doesn't have to preclude the others. Let's find our meanings where we can.[6]

Given that desire, let's explore perhaps the two most important concepts that Superman can teach us about religion, the idea of the elevated or enlightened being and the Christian concept of Incarnation. Like Neo (Keanu Reeves) in the *Matrix* films, Superman is the One, the perfect combination of divine power and human spirit who can save his society. The very name Superman takes on resonance here. Unlike German philosopher

Friedrich Nietzsche's *übermensch* ("overman"), Kal-El's power does not elevate him above humanity. He represents instead a sort of culmination of human achievement, and despite his alien origin and unearthly powers, he considers himself to be very human. So, like Jesus, or like the Buddha, Kal-El is an elevated human who represents a model for us, a model not only of strength, but of decency, not only of power, but also of moral authority.

In Jeph Loeb's rendering of Kal-El in *A Superman for All Seasons*, we can see the mingling of humanity and power that leads us at last to think of the central mystery of the Christian faith: the incarnation, Emanu-El, God with Us. Loeb makes clear to us what was sometimes lost by the Superman writers of the 1950s through the 1980s, and what is sometimes lost on Christians today: for incarnation to be real, this savior must be equally God and man.

In the chapter of *A Superman for All Seasons* narrated by Clark Kent's childhood friend and love, Lana Lang, it becomes clear that Superman is who he is both because of his human history and his alien destiny. He is more than a set of super-powers impersonally slopping up evil; he is a person of great love and compassion, informed by his human qualities even as he uses his superpowers to set things right. "People wondered why anyone with those powers and abilities—if it were true—would use them to help others and not for their own benefit," Lana muses. "To understand that man in the cape who could fly—all I needed to know was Clark."[7]

Here, at the incarnation, is where many Christians have got-ten Christ wrong over the years. In the early years of the Chris-tian church, there was continuous wrangling over the nature of Christ, about how human he was or how God-like, about whether he was a human who became a God or a part of God from the beginning of time, and on and on. The Council of Nicaea, which in 325 produced the Nicene Creed often used in Christian worship, sent those who followed the Arian belief—that Christ was not fully God from the beginning of time—to the showers. Likewise, those who believed in the Marcionite heresy—that Jesus was never fully human—were ultimately disappointed as well. The Council of Chalcedon in 451 outlined incarnation in the following way, and if this seems a little legalistic, remember that we're talking about a great controversy that people were trying to resolve. Not every Christian will agree wholeheartedly with the council's conclusions, but it does provide us with a clear definition of who and what Jesus was. Because of that, it's worth our reading and understanding:

> Truly God and truly man, consisting also of a reasonable soul and body; of one substance with the Father as regards his Godhead, and at the same time of one substance with us as regards his manhood; like us in all respects, apart from sin . . . begotten of the Father before the ages, but . . . begotten, for us men and for our salvation, of Mary the Virgin, the God-bearer . . . the characteristics of each nature being preserved and coming together to form one person.[8]

When we think about Superman, it shouldn't be in the cynical way that Nietzsche expressed the concept, as one who would be over others and use his power however he wanted; Hitler took this philosophy to its logical and horrifying extension. Instead, we can see it like this: Super/Man, a combination of that which is greater than human (the divine, in the case of Jesus) and that which makes us completely human coming together in one person. Just as Loeb's Kal-El saves others with his supernatural power channeled by his human impulses, the Christian Emanu-El performs many of his miracles out of his human love and compassion—the wine for the wedding feast, the healings, and perhaps most obviously, the raising of his friend Lazarus from the dead.

It's obvious if you think about it for a second that Jesus couldn't go around raising every dead person; it wouldn't be good policy for lots of reasons. But Lazarus was not only the brother of the sisters Mary and Martha, whom Jesus loved, but was beloved of Jesus himself. The Gospel of John tells us that when Jesus heard the news, he wept, and out of his full range of human emotions—anger and sorrow and love and compassion—he performed a miracle that married his human and God natures: he turned back the forces of death and decay and gave his friend new life:

> Mary came to where Jesus was waiting and fell at his feet, saying, "Master, if only you had been here, my brother would not have died."
> When Jesus saw her sobbing and the Jews with her sobbing, a deep anger welled up within him. He said, "Where did you put him?"
> "Master, come and see," they said. Now Jesus wept.
> The Jews said, "Look how deeply he loved him."
> Others among them said, "Well, if he loved him so much, why didn't he do something to keep him from dying? After all, he opened the eyes of a blind man."
> Then Jesus, the anger again welling up within him, arrived at the tomb. It was a simple cave in the hillside with a slab of stone laid against it. Jesus said, "Remove the stone." . . .
> Then he shouted, "Lazarus, come out!" And he came out, a cadaver, wrapped from head to toe, and with a kerchief over his face.[9]

In the one-shot comic *Superman vs. Darkseid: Apokolips Now!* Superman illustrates these principles in a way startlingly similar to this miracle of Lazarus. At the outset of the magazine, Nat, the niece of the superhero known as Steel, sets the stage by saying, "I was raised to believe that love and commitment and personal responsibility hold us all together. . . . I know Superman believes that too. I know he believes that if you save one life, you save the world. I know he would go to the ends of the universe for a friend."[10]

This statement of Superman's beliefs weds Jewish and Christian teachings in a beautiful way. The Talmudic wisdom "He who saves one life saves the world entire" joins John 15:13, "Greater love hath no man than this, that a man lay down his life for his friends." These lines could form a core morality for most comic superheroes: every life is worth saving, even at the risk of one's own.

In this story, Superman grapples with the god of evil, Dark-seid, in the hell-world called Apokolips for the power to resur-rect his friend John Henry Irons/Steel. It is an epic battle (as is the Christian story of the Harrowing of Hell, Christ's descent into hell following his death on the cross), which ends in his victory. At story's end, Nat has confirmed Superman's heroism, but it has also encouraged her own: "Bottom line, he changed my life. My life will count for something. I WILL make a dif-ference. I will work to change the world."[11]

This is an essential bit of wisdom we can learn from comics. Not everyone can be a Superman. But as Nat points out in *Superman vs. Darkseid,* the exploits of Superman (like the lesson of Jesus) shouldn't simply evoke a passive, Gee whiz! sort of response. They should be a call to better ourselves, to save oth-ers, to set them free in their bodies, minds, and souls. As *Super-man* writer Kurt Busiek notes, Superman is always relevant: he's a model for us "every time we wish we could do something noble."[12] In fact, he has, from his beginnings, been a model for us. Bryan Singer liked how Superman "helped out, but he pri-marily led by example. He stirred others; he inspired. He left the actual heroism to the real heroes, to the soldiers in the field and abroad, and in that way, he became this very inspiring figure."[13]

The writers and artists of other comic book saviors have consciously built on the Christian archetype. As I was planning this book, Andrew Arnold, the comics writer from Time.com, reminded me of one of those examples, the more than slightly heavy-handed Christian symbolism of the Marvel character Adam Warlock, who was crucified before coming back to life; the messianic aspects of this universal savior were much better handled in story lines from the 1970s to the present by War-lock artist and writer Jim Starlin. But perhaps not only because Superman was the first but also because the elements of his character were drawn from the needs of his creators, he contin-ues to be the most powerful example. In the years to come, as new movies, comics, computer games, and other media ver-sions of this made-for-comics messiah come into our lives, let's remember the model for advancement Superman gives us, the understanding of the divine he represents for us. And let's remember the idea of a savior who comes to help us become who we're supposed to be.

We can't all be Superman. But we can be better men and women, working to change the world.

With Great Power Comes Great Responsibility

Lois Lane: Oh come on. You're—
   Superman: No different from anybody else who uses the
gifts God gave them to help people.
                    —*Adventures of Superman*, February 2004

One of the seminal moments in modern popular culture came
in the spring of 1962, when an unlikely hero saw the light of
day in the last issue of a discontinued comics magazine called
Amazing Fantasy. The hero was a troubled teenager named
Peter Parker who received strange powers as the result of a
radioactive spider's bite, and the series almost never saw the
light of day because it violated almost every rule about superheroes that had come down from the mountain with Kal-El.
Spider-Man's cocreator Stan Lee toted up some of them: "You
can't feature a teenager as a super hero. Teenagers can only be
sidekicks. . . . You can't give a hero so many problems. Readers
won't think he's heroic enough. . . . You can't have a hero who
isn't big and glamorous and handsome."[1]
   Peter Parker—in and out of costume—was like lots of the
people who made up his audience. He read too much; he wasn't
built like Arnold Schwarzenegger; he lived with his aunt and
uncle in a plain-Jane American neighborhood. He wasn't glamorous: he wasn't a test pilot, or a reporter, or a billionaire philanthropist, or an Amazon princess. But let's face it: when we look in
the mirror in the morning, very few of us see a millionaire indus-

trialist who fights crime in his secret identity. Spider-Man appeals to us so much because he is like us, just an ordinary person who happened to have something extraordinary change his life—and had to face the consequences and make choices arising from it.

Spider-Man ushered in the Silver Age of comics, marked by a new realism and heroes who were imperfect but also more like us. If the radioactive spider that empowered Peter Parker had bitten one of us, we would have faced the same challenges and temptations he faces. Because of that kinship, Peter's most important lesson, which came in the last issue of *Amazing Fantasy*, resonates even these many years later, both in comics and in its straight retelling in the first *Spider-Man* (one of the most popular films in history).

When that spider bites high school bookworm Peter Parker, he discovers that he has received powers beyond those of ordinary mortals. He can cling to walls, leap prodigious distances, lift large things over his head. What does he do with that power?

Well, at first he does what a lot of us would do: he uses that power for his own benefit. After defeating a professional wrestler with his newfound abilities, he performs on television. As he leaves the TV studio, a burglar rushes toward him, pursued by a police officer, but although Peter could stop him easily, he lets him reach the elevator and escape.

"What's with you, mister?" asks the police officer. "All you hadda do was trip him, or hold him just for a minute."

Peter brushes him off. "I'm through being pushed around," he says. "From now on I just look out for number one."[2]

And he does, pursuing fame and wealth with his newfound power. But one evening, he returns home to find police cars parked in front of his home. His Uncle Ben has been killed by a burglar he surprised, and when Spider-Man tracks the crook to an abandoned warehouse, he captures him—and learns something that changes his life.

The burglar who killed his uncle is the same crook he earlier allowed to escape because he didn't want to be bothered.

Devastated, Peter realizes that his selfish use of his power has had horrible consequences; if he'd used his power more constructively, his uncle would still be alive. In the final panel of *Amazing Fantasy* #15, a forlorn Peter passes down a darkened street beneath the full moon, "aware at last that in the world, with great power there must also come—great responsibility!"[3] In the first *Spider-Man* film, a montage of Peter performing good deeds shows his acceptance of that message.

Peter learns what power is, how it should be used, and the consequences of misusing it. And while we can see this story of accountability replayed throughout the history of comics, it's the Spider-Man story that I want to focus on first, because it is so close to our own experience. What would we do if we received some kind of power? And more important, what should we do?

Peter's story tells us.

This isn't, by the way, just some sort of abstract intellectual exercise, because although none of us is going to be bitten by a radioactive spider, many of us have or are going to receive power of some kind and have to decide how to use it. In fact, at this moment most of us have power beyond that of most people on the earth—we just haven't realized it.

What is power? Power is the ability to influence events, exercise your will, make things happen. In superhero comics, power is raw and elemental: to fly, bend iron bars, punch out a hundred bad guys. But at its core, power is all the same: the ability to influence your environment to the outcomes you desire. In comics, it may be Green Lantern's ability to create any sort of construct he can envision and his willpower can maintain; it may be the Punisher's ability to shoot faster and straighter than his underworld foes; it may be Morpheus/Dream/Sandman and his abilities to shape the dreams of mortals. But in life, power comes in many forms.

The president of the United States is routinely called the most powerful man on earth. That power comes in part from America's military might—the technological achievements of our weapons designers, the well-trained troops—the sort of raw force that leads to the simplistic solution of violence. But America's power comes from many other sources, including its wealth and economic power. When a nation that represents only one twentieth of the world's population has the wealth to consume one fourth of its resources, each one of us partakes of a power that billions of people in the world can only imagine.

Power can be used for good or ill, and it can be hard sometimes to figure out which is which, especially when someone has something approaching absolute power. Lord Acton famously said, "Power corrupts; absolute power corrupts absolutely." Some years ago in a run of Marvel's *The Mighty Thor*, the Norse god of thunder decided that since he had the power to solve the problems of the world, he would, whether people wanted him to or not. It created a number of interesting stories; some people were drawn to Thor's naked exercise of power and others repelled by it. An underground even grew up to fight Thor's benign use of power, something that Thor himself had difficulty in understanding. In the Superman miniseries *Red Son*, writer Mark Millar examined a seemingly blasphemous question: What if Superman had landed in a Russian wheat field instead of an American one? Then how would his use of power—and the political ideologies to which he gave that power—have resulted in a different world? Would he have been a different hero?

The very title of Brian Michael Bendis's *Powers* points to a central conflict considered in this superhero police procedural. Detective Christian Walker, who used to have superpowers, now tries to bring justice in cases involving superheroes. When a hero gets murdered, a supervillain must be taken into custody, or when a hero goes rogue, Walker is called in.

An ongoing subtext in the book is how people with power(s) affect the lives of those who don't have them. Some, of course, are grateful for the protection and relative safety they receive because of the heroes in tights; others question whether their beneficial rule is as benign as it seems. In one story arc, a group of antihero vigilantes attempt to kill superheroes (including Walker, even though at that time he no longer has powers), because, they argue, by delegating moral authority to these costumed heroes, society is setting itself up to be taken over or destroyed by those with power. At this time (before Marvel's "Civil War" over superhero registration), it was a radical notion for comics, even after the cautionary tales in *Watchmen* and *Dark Knight* and Green Lantern's turn to the dark side.

But in a later *Powers* story arc, one of the world's most powerful superheroes goes rogue and destroys the pope, levels the West Bank, and threatens to enforce his version of order over the entire world simply because he believes himself to be as superior to others as they have always believed him to be. It's a startling vision of what could happen when people collaborate in a group delusion that might inevitably makes right.

In our own lives, the questions can be taken back to Peter Parker's initial realization. If you are reading these words, then chances are you control more power, just by being a typical American—political, technological, and economic power, if not cosmic or physical or magical—than almost everyone else in the world. So how do we behave responsibly with that power?

The full answer would probably require another book, but there are some simple answers that can make a beginning. In the Hebrew Bible, the book of Micah tells us to pursue justice:

> He's already made it plain how to live, what to do,
>   what GOD is looking for in men and women.
> It's quite simple: Do what is fair and just to your neighbor,
>   be compassionate and loyal in your love,
> And don't take yourself too seriously—
>   take God seriously.[4]

That gives us a beginning we'll expand in the next chapter; by contrast, the Catholic monastic writer Thomas Merton defines a Christian view of what it is we *shouldn't* further with our power: "inequality, injustice, [anything] which seeks more for myself than my rights allow, and which gives others less than they should receive."[5] So by extension, using our power unselfishly and responsibly means considering others, seeking equality and justice, giving others what they need.

In the Gospels, Jesus delivers some ultimate lessons about power—what it's for, what it isn't for. In the story of his temptation by Satan, which appears in several of the Gospels, Jesus is challenged to use his power to satisfy himself: to turn stones to bread to sate his hunger, to toss himself from the top of the Temple to prove to others that he is especially favored by God and no harm will come to him. But Jesus disdains those petty parlor tricks; he says that power was given to him for other reasons, and in the King James translation of Mark 2:10–11, we hear Jesus saying to a sick man (and a crowd of skeptical observers), "But that ye may know that the Son of man hath power on earth to forgive sins . . . I say unto thee, Arise, and take up thy bed, and go thy way into thine house."

Jesus used his supernatural power of healing to demonstrate his spiritual power to forgive. Both powers were powers of compassion, of service, of creating a whole world out of broken people. Elsewhere, we find Jesus telling his listeners how the precepts we've just read from Micah and Thomas Merton might be put into effect, how their own power might be best used. In a story about ultimate judgment from the Gospel of Matthew, Jesus said that the people who embodied the kingdom of God were those who could recognize themselves in the following:

> I was hungry and you fed me,
> I was thirsty and you gave me a drink,
> I was homeless and you gave me a room,
> I was shivering and you gave me clothes,
> I was sick and you stopped to visit,
> I was in prison and you came to me.[6]

So here's the ultimate lesson on power: if you want to be blessed, you must use your power to protect and defend those less fortunate. As Archbishop Desmond Tutu points out, it's the very heart of Jesus' message in the New Testament and God's prophets in the Hebrew Bible, the heart of what power is and what it should do:

> The God we worship is the same yesterday, today, and forever. That God knows, that God hears, that God sees, and that God will come down to deliver his people. . . . The God we worship is not a God who is neutral. Our God is a

God who takes sides. Our God is a God who takes the side of the poor, of the oppressed, of the downtrodden, and that is where the Church of God must be found. The Church of God must be the voice of the voiceless ones. The Church of God must be with the poor, the homeless, the naked and the hungry.[7]

So how should heroes use their power? Maybe we can't rescue people from a volcano or stop bullets with our bare hands. But we can be heroes by saving others in less obvious ways. We can extend compassion and kindness to those within our circle, and we can reach out and project our power into the world to do good. In practical terms, that could mean charity or volunteerism; it could mean adopting orphans from a third-world country or donating from our abundance to fight the AIDS crisis in Africa; it could mean political action to achieve justice for migrant workers in Bangladesh or boycotts of stores that sell clothing made in sweatshops.

But whatever we choose, it does require a new consciousness. We are not, as human beings, naturally responsible. We are, in fact, largely selfish. When Peter Parker decides to give up his Spider-Man identity in *Spider-Man II*, or when he lets his desires for acceptance and revenge almost overwhelm him in *Spider-Man III*, he is not behaving with great responsibility. Instead he's behaving just like the rest of us. But as faith traditions from Buddhism to Islam to Christianity remind us, a compassion for others must constantly be cultivated, because the consequences for failing to be compassionate are so serious. In one of his sermons, Dr. Martin Luther King Jr. said, "Much of the evil which we experience is caused by man's folly and ignorance and also by the misuse of his freedom."[8]

Like Peter Parker, we are regular people who discover that we have the power to make the world better; we also have the power to make it worse.

And because we have power, we have great responsibility.

Truth, Justice,
and the American Way

God offers to everyone his choice between truth and repose.
Take which you please—you can never have both.
　　　　　　　　　　　　　　　　　—Ralph Waldo Emerson

At the beginning of every one of those black-and-white Superman television shows from the 1950s we are reminded that Big
Blue fights for "truth, justice, and the American way." It was
then, and remains, a summary of the morality most comic
book heroes follow, but few people then or now have ever
stopped to think about what those words mean. Perhaps they
have thought these words were transparent, but in truth, they
mean whatever we want them to, and are shaped by our
already-held beliefs and prejudices. We think we know, for
example, what truth is: it's all very well for young John Grady
Cole—the main character of Cormac McCarthy's novel *All the
Pretty Horses*, and himself so capable he's a sort of Western
superhero—to say in that pragmatically American way, "There
ain't but one truth. . . . The truth is what happened."[1]

But the truth is, the truth itself is subjective. It's not for
nothing that the writer of John's Gospel records Pontius Pilate
asking Jesus, "What is truth?"

Since comics heroes got their genesis in America, they are
simultaneously universal and parochial. We've seen how they

35

draw on archetypal stories and heroes from across the generations and the globe. At the same time, they came to life, many
of them, in a certain place, at a certain time: in the late 1930s
and early 1940s in an America struggling through the Great
Depression and entering a worldwide battle against fascism,
World War II. Because of this, the underlying principles of
many of these early comics heroes reflect universal principles of
morality found in the Hebrew Bible and the New Testament,
but also peculiarly American notions of right and wrong,
wrapped in patriotism. In this chapter, we'll look at some of the
major heroes, the beliefs they espouse, and the ways that even
today they—and we—struggle to do the right thing.

TRUTH

What is truth? It's a seemingly simple question that Pilate posed
to Jesus. So why is it that philosophers and theologians have
been asking it continually for thousands of years? One problem
comes because we confuse two things: truth and Truth. Our
experiences come in ways that seem to us like unfiltered reality,
but we all know that two people can see the same situation in a
very different way because of the filters we have in place.

This leads us to the idea that many "truths" are subjective;
what I see, or hear, or believe, may not match your memory or
perception of the same event. At the same time, the truths that
come to us from the larger world, whether we call them "news"
or "history," are also coming through a set of interpretive filters.
If a bomb goes off in the Middle East, CNN, Fox News, and
Arab news networks may report the reasons for it and the reper-
cussions of it differently. It's essential that we weigh and balance,
that we try to broaden the sources of our understanding of
truth, because as Martin Luther King Jr. noticed, "Few people
realize that even our authentic channels of information—the
press, the platform, and in many cases, the pulpit—do not give
us objective and unbiased truth."[2] So before we make decisions
about right and wrong, about how to act, the question has to

expand beyond "What is truth?" It has to become "Whose truth is this? And can I accept it as mine?"

The philosopher William James suggested a set of considerations we might undertake before we apprehend something to be true. James suggested that "those statements and theories are true that do all the jobs required of them: first and foremost, fit all the known facts, accord with other well-attested statements and scientific laws of experience, but also withstand criticism, suggest useful insights, yield accurate predictions."[3]

This view may be a bit reductive—we may want to think that truth is more than simply what stands up to such testing, that it proceeds from some fount of absolute truth or reality. But this seems like a useful starting point. Certainly it's a process that truth ought to go through before it becomes Truth, the sort of knowledge or belief at the heart of who we are and what we do. And, unfortunately, it often doesn't; as expressed so well by comic book scribes the Wachowski brothers in *The Matrix*, we often simply accept the truths passed down to us uncritically, without measuring them for ourselves, without asking the questions. Chris Seay and I wrote in *The Gospel Reloaded*,

> The question is more important than the answer. Or more importantly, asking ourselves the question(s) is more important than our accepting without question an answer—any answer. What holds us back, restrains our ambition, and silences our potential? The unthinking, unreasoning, unquestioning acceptance of anything.[4]

This seems to me to be a Truth, but if it is, it's a postmodern one, and one that would have seemed very alien to Americans of the early twentieth century. Most of them held certain truths to be self-evident: America was a country full of decent, hard-working people who stood in stark opposition and contrast to the fascists in Germany and Italy and Japan. Watching the "Why We Fight" documentary film series directed by Hollywood producer and director Frank Capra in the early years of World War II is like opening a time capsule into a world of simpler beliefs and communal truths: Americans valued the square deal, fairness, equality (at least in theory); supported religious freedom (for the most part); and believed that everyone could get ahead if they were smart enough or worked hard enough. They believed in freedom and justice for all, believed God chose them for some great purpose (as we'll discuss later in the chapter), and were absolutely, positively dead sure that they were right.

It may have been one of the few times in history that being absolutely, positively sure you were right turned out to be a good thing instead of a bad one. As we'll see in a moment, oftentimes surety can be more dangerous than any enemy you face. But in the 1930s and 1940s, for once the world really did boil down into camps that could be outlined in black and wide. The Germans and the Japanese were exploiters willing to destroy anyone they considered less perfect than themselves (which is to say that they were absolutely, positively sure that *they* were right). There was right and there was wrong; there was good and there was evil.

And into this world came the heroes.

From the very beginning, with the possible exception of Batman (who has always seemed a bit dark and disturbing to some people with his unswerving drive toward justice), comics represented a very clear-cut vision of truth. There were the heroes: Superman, Captain Marvel, the Atom, Hawkman, Wonder Woman, the Flash, the Ray, Green Lantern, Doll Man, the Shield, Captain America. And then, arrayed against them were the bank robbers and jewel thieves, the mad scientists, the inscrutable Oriental geniuses scheming world domination, the criminal masterminds, and finally, Hitler, Mussolini, and the Japanese militarists themselves. And there was no need for soul-searching or moral equivocation. The heroes were good; the villains were bad.

After the war, our heroes continued to fight evil head-on, two-fisted, sure of their continued rightness. But as the civil rights movement fermented and spilled into the streets, as fights for economic justice began to rage, and as Americans began to recognize how the flag-draped excesses of the McCarthy hearings and the House Un-American Activities Committee ruined lives and shattered careers, often on rumors and innuendo, the simple black-and-white vision of America seemed increasingly outdated, and the simple black-and-white morality of our superheroes seemed increasingly outmoded. It's no wonder that the 1960s TV version of Batman was a camp parody of simple superhero morality; to an increasingly hip and savvy populace, the old verities didn't seem to hold so much truth anymore.

But one of the responses to a more complicated world is often an attempt on the part of some people to hold onto a truth—to make it the Truth—ever more strongly. In *The Battle for God: A History of Fundamentalism*, theologian Karen Armstrong has written cogently about this way of thinking, which has emerged in response to a crisis: a world of continuing change and complication. Since they fear that they and their way of life are going to be wiped off the earth, some people fortify their identities by a selective return to doctrines and beliefs that make sense of the world for them.[5] Whether we speak of Christian, Jewish, or Islamic fundamentalists—or even of secular fundamentalists, who might like to return America to the policies or social climate of the 1950s (or the 1850s)—we are talking about people who tend to believe that they hold the Truth.

And while this might be a valuable thing in thinking of a war against an absolute evil or a comic book conflict against villains such as the Red Skull, Lex Luthor, or the Joker, the world is rarely so simply black and white. Charles Kimball has identified a series of warning signs that indicate when belief can become dangerous, and the first of them just happens to be the belief that you and your fellow believers—and you only— hold the absolute truth. Others follow quickly—blind obedience, end justifying the means, and ultimately, "holy war."[6] Even sincere believers—whether people of faith, or nationalists, or advocates of social justice or free trade—are susceptible to this kind of damaging adherence to the Truth, which divides the world into us and them and closes our eyes to the possibility that anyone else may have anything useful to teach us.

It took a long time for mainstream comics to advance beyond this simple black-and-white morality and vision of truth, perhaps partly because they were written largely for kids during most of that time. During the 1960s and 1970s, the occasional comic would directly or indirectly complicate our understanding of the world. *Uncanny X-Men* (and, today, its thousand spin-offs) has always served as a continuing symbolic rebuttal of prevailing attitudes on race and other prejudices; issues of *Green Lantern and Green Arrow* raised the question of why superheroes no longer confronted real world problems like racial and economic injustice. At last, landmark works like *Watchmen* questioned traditional truths about "truth, justice, and the American way." And today, we live in a world where our popular culture often acknowledges the complex nature of that world.

In the *Identity Crisis* story line featuring the greatest heroes of the DC universe, the Justice League of America, writer Brad Meltzer explored the consequences of inconvenient truths and outright lies, particularly those told by heroes. For years, members of the League had kept from Batman the information that long ago they had not only altered the personality of the villainous Dr. Light to make him less of a menace (a sort of magical lobotomy), but they had also erased the Batman's memory of their act since he violently opposed it. When Dr. Light regained his memory—and Batman figured out what had happened to both of them—this white lie broke up the Justice League and sowed distrust among the world's heroes. When word got out that they had "brain wiped" not only villains but their own ally, the news caused the heroes to be regarded as little better than the criminals they opposed. This failure in the matter of truth also turned out, ultimately, to be a question of justice.

JUSTICE

What is justice? Most of us, particularly in regard to comic book morality, tend to think of justice in terms that are purely punitive: the justice system, the Justice League of America, the

Justice Society of America. In comics, somebody does a bad thing: the Riddler robs a bank, the Red Skull brandishes an atomic device, Thanos threatens to destroy the universe. The story line then follows the pursuit of retributive justice: the miscreant is captured, contained, or destroyed—obliteration is our favorite dramatic fate for villains—and justice is served.

Batman, one of the most mythically potent of comic characters, has always been the foremost example of this punitive understanding of justice. The tagline for the current Batman series explains his motivation in this way: "I made a promise on the grave of my parents to rid this city of the evil that took their lives." Over the years, Batman has been depicted as driven solely by his concern for retributive justice. After witnessing the death of his parents at the hands of a small-time hood, Bruce Wayne has devoted his entire existence to the pursuit and punishment of evil. As a young man, he travels the world seeking mental and physical training, and devotes himself to the study of forensic science and detective work. As an adult, he lives only to fight crime.

That drive—rendered by some writers, as we'll see, as obsession—leads him to a vision of justice that permits few gray areas. Although Alan Moore, a master of ambiguity, created a Batman in *The Killing Joke* who seems willing to consider societal and psychological determinants, this is a Batman outside the mainstream. As Frank Miller says, "I disagree with everything [Moore] did in that book. . . . My Joker was more evil than troubled; Alan's was more troubled than evil."[7] In other recent views of the Batman, whether Miller's Dark Knight or Jeph Loeb's recent chart-topping version of the Caped Crusader, he remains sure of himself, sure of his methods, and unwilling to change, bend, or move.

In the graphic novel *Absolution*, one of the most spiritual of comic writers, J. M. DeMatteis, depicts a Batman who believes that perhaps there was once a Presence who created the universe, "but a bearded Creator sitting on his throne—judging souls and dispensing justice?"[8] No; that is the job that Batman has to perform, and in the process, he has no room for the idea that criminals can change, that people can grow, that a terrorist could amend her life and become a force for good.

The Christian ideal of redemption is alien to Batman in *Absolution*; he refuses even to consider the possibility that the terrorist he is pursuing, Jennifer Blake, might have found a way to repay society for her past crimes. There is only one way to dispense justice for her terrorist attack on Bruce Wayne's employees, and Batman cannot be tempted by appeals to his feelings. "I learned long ago," he says, "that Satan isn't some horned tempter standing in a lake of fire. . . . The devil is our own will when it weakens, our mind when it gives way to the illogic of the heart."[9]

Justice, then, is a matter of the head, not the heart, and there is no room for emotion in its administration. The Batman who fears a relationship with Catwoman, who prides himself on being a cold, methodical thinking machine, represents a vision of justice that is appealing to us in troubling times. Evil exists in the world, and it needs to be countered by an implacable foe. But as many writers have pointed out, Batman's success as a crime fighter has come at the expense of his success as a fully rounded human being. He reminds us in some ways of Victor Hugo's Inspector Javert, the relentless justice machine who serves as the antagonist of *Les Misérables*. When confronted with the complicated idea of redemption as opposed to simple retributive justice, Inspector Javert shorts out like one of those troubled computers on the old *Star Trek* show, and sometimes we sense that Batman is one lightbulb over his head away from a breakdown.

In the cosmology of comics, Batman represents a version of God sometimes attributed to the books of the Hebrew Bible, the "Old Testament" God of retribution and harsh justice. (In naming a 2003 miniseries *Trinity*, DC Comics finally acknowledged that in the persons of Batman, Superman, and Wonder Woman they had a fully functional equivalent of the Christian trinity of Father, Son, and Holy Spirit.) This "Old Testament" vision doesn't do justice to the true Hebrew idea of justice, however, which goes far beyond "an eye for an eye," and which opens new vistas for us as we think about the concept.

Justice is more than punishment, a response to a negative action; it is also righteousness, a response to negative conditions. To think of justice simply as retribution and punishment for crimes committed is entirely too limiting; just as the Anglican Book of Common Prayer's confession includes sins of commission, it also includes those things that we ought to have done, but didn't.

The Batman in *Batman Begins* gives us perhaps our healthiest view of justice—both what it is, and what it is not. Early in the film, Bruce Wayne (Christian Bale) waits outside a courtroom to murder the man who killed his parents. But when he is confronted by the example of his childhood friend Rachel (Katie Holmes), who becomes a district attorney, and discovers that he can't easily accept the implacable teachings of his mentor that one must "do what is necessary to defeat evil," Bruce/Batman draws the line. This Batman may use the darkness and fear as his methods, but he understands that justice is not—and cannot be—simply about personal revenge. It must be something more.

He also sees that he has a responsibility to pursue justice by night and by day—that in fact his work as Bruce Wayne, billionaire philanthropist, may be at least as important as the work of his dark alter ego. His father invested in the community of Gotham City because he believed in it and wanted to fight crime, poverty, and misery. And that work of positive justice is a powerful example we often forget when we imagine what justice might be.

The Hebrew word *tzedek*, which is sometimes translated in the Bible as "justice," may also be translated as "charity" or "righteousness." As John Ziesler points out, while "righteous" may mean someone or something proven in a judicial context, it is more widely applied to moral character: "The scope of righteousness is much wider than judicial procedures and embraces the whole covenanted life under God."[10]

The Hebrew prophets—and the teachings of Jesus—continually reinforce the idea of justice as social and economic justice. In the book of Deuteronomy, people are ordered to "pursue justice," while in Micah 6:8, a central text in Jewish belief, justice is made one of the three basic tenets of Jewish monotheism. Rabbi Joseph Telushkin writes that the "pursuit of justice, an obsession with doing good deeds, and humility" are the hallmarks of a godly person.[11] Also sounds a little like your traditional superhero, doesn't it?

Jesus likewise boils belief down to loving God and loving our neighbors as ourselves; in telling the illustrative parable of the Good Samaritan, he tells us that all people—even those who hate us—are our neighbors, and that it is our responsibility to treat them with kindness, concern, and charity. Since every major faith tradition has its own version of the Golden Rule, it's clear that every ethical system believes this expanded form of justice—doing what's right—is necessary if we're going to live together in peace.

In the early days of comics, Superman demonstrated this broad concern for justice by fighting slumlords as well as bank robbers. As comics historian Les Daniels has noted, "It almost went without saying that [Superman] would catch crooks, prevent disasters and impress women. What was remarkable about Superman is that [writer Jerry] Siegel gave this fantasy figure a serious social conscience. In his earliest adventures, Superman was a reformer."[12] In some of these formative issues, Superman rescues a victim from a lynch mob, confronts a greedy mine owner, convenes a peace conference, punishes a wife beater, and fights corruption in the U.S. government. (And in the 1999 graphic novel by Paul Dini and Alex Ross, *Superman: Peace on Earth*, Superman returns to his roots by undertaking a noble, if futile, attempt to end world hunger.) But somewhere along the way, that radical concern for victims of societal evils got lost, and for most of comics history, justice has been purely a matter of fisticuffs and apprehending the bad guys.

For that reason, it's refreshing to find postmodern titles like *The Authority* and Brian Michael Bendis's *Daredevil* suggesting that heroes need to wrestle with the root causes of poverty and injustice instead of simply accepting the status quo and dealing with the occasional aberrant manifestation of evil. A concern for the poor and deprived is at the heart of Judaism, Christianity, and Islam alike, and social justice, broadly defined, means an ongoing movement toward equal opportunities for all people, and support for the less privileged, aged, or infirm.

This form of justice represents a truly radical message, often unsettling to those in power or positions of privilege (which, incidentally, is most of us with the leisure and the resources to read comics and see movies). But to seek justice without pursuing it for everyone is impossible in the long run. Martin Luther King Jr. often spoke about how the church, if it preached good spiritual deeds but not good works, would become an irrelevant social club, while Archbishop Desmond Tutu, in his own fight against racism and injustice, told audiences that for Jesus and all those coming from the Jewish tradition, "God's liberation would have to have real consequences in the political, social, and economic spheres or it was no Gospel at all."[13] We have only to remember Superman's early exploits to remind ourselves that Jesus was a social reformer as well as a godlike redeemer.

Bottom line: the world needs to be a better place for all of us. In a cosmic sense, it doesn't matter if we put the bank robbers or murderers behind bars if there are still people starving, shivering, or suffering under the heels of oppression. As Dr. King often said in speeches and sermons, "Injustice anywhere is a threat to justice everywhere."

It's a tall order; not just to find the bad guys, but to fix the bad things about our world. All of them.

A tall order.

But certainly it's worth the attempt.

THE AMERICAN WAY

We have always considered patriotism to be one of the primary attributes of American superheroes. Partly this was a result of how closely the coming of World War II and America's struggle for survival followed on the heels of the creation of Superman, Batman, and the others, but there are other reasons. Superman, raised as a farm boy in the American heartland, has often been depicted bearing an American flag over the years; Wonder Woman almost wears a flag, with her star-spangled red, white, and blue costume; the coming of the war saw Batman selling war bonds on comic book covers and Captain America and other new heroes fighting Nazis inside the covers.

With the possible exception of Superman, Captain America is the comic character most closely identified with patriotism and nationalism, unsurprising given his origins. Steve Rogers, a sickly but patriotic young man, was so upset at being denied the opportunity to serve in World War II that he volunteered for a secret project: to be injected with the Super Soldier formula. The experiment was a success: Steve Rogers became a physical specimen developed to the limits of human possibility. After being trained in tactics and combat, he was given a red, white, and blue uniform and a shield, and christened Captain America.

Cap fought the Nazis throughout World War II, and was even brought back to life to fight communists for a short time in the 1950s, but his greatest success was when he was revived in the pages of a fledgling superhero title published by Marvel Comics called *The Avengers* and was restored to the modern world. Captain America has since become one of Marvel's signature characters, the moral heart of the Avengers in its many incarnations over the past forty years, and the star of his own long-running solo book.

He also became, according to Robert Jewett and John Shelton Lawrence, a pop culture symbol of what they call "zealous nationalism" (partial justice) as opposed to "prophetic realism" (impartial justice). While their recent book *Captain America and the Crusade against Evil* may oversimplify Captain America's legacy somewhat, their primary thesis is persuasive: that through examining Captain America's actions and character over many years, we can see reflected America's own actions and character and our struggle with what Jewett and Lawrence call "the challenge of pop fascism."

In *Captain America* and most other superhero comics, we have often seen this vision of American "pop fascism." The traditional superhero myth suggests that power in one set of capable hands is the surest way to achieve justice, that democratic systems can't be trusted to perform their tasks alone, that the hero would never take advantage of those he serves, and that the world requires American superheroism.[14]

It's a startling thought that in one of the world's most democratic nations we have formulated this myth of benevolent fascism—and have even extended it to our own foreign policy. The world needs us, we tell ourselves; we are, so to speak, the world's only superheroes, and without us, the democratic mechanisms in place to deal with the world's problems will fail.

So it's useful for us to remind ourselves of the democratic traditions at the heart of the American way, and of what the image of Captain America can also stand for besides a sort of narrow-minded belief that Americans command a monopoly on truth and justice. First, it's heartening to remember that American beliefs are essentially democratic and inspired: that all people are entitled to equal justice and that the American creed is a "union of faith and freedom, in which faith elevates freedom and freedom tempers faith."[15]

Lord Chesterton famously called America "a nation with the soul of a church," which is both good and bad. Americans have long had the sense that in some ways they were doing God's work on earth, and when the American way has matched the broad ideas of truth and justice we've discussed in this chapter, America has been a force for good, fighting against greed, poverty, repression, and ignorance around the globe.

But when we have been convinced of our own rightness— that whatever we did would be true and just because we're America—we've sometimes exploited other peoples, inserted ourselves in the governance of sovereign nations, and been an agent not of good, but of evil. Being American is, unfortunately, no guarantee of doing the right thing, although we hope because of our democratic institutions and high ideals that we will do right more often than not.

Jewett and Lawrence argue that simple jingoistic patriotism—American might makes right—is at the heart of the Captain America character, and certainly that might have been true of him in his World War II and early Marvel incarnations. One can almost imagine the original Cap putting an "America, Love It or Leave It" bumper sticker on his shield before going out to bust some heads. But at least since the 1970s, in his own title and in *The Avengers*, Captain America has stood up to patriots who also espoused racism or violence, questioned the nation's governance during the Watergate era, and most recently, asked hard questions about the American way—and about the policies that have made that way possible over the years.

In the dark days just after the September 11 bombings, in fact, *Captain America* presented the extremely unpopular idea that people around the world might have been made angry enough to kill Americans as a result of our own actions and interventions in their affairs over the years, while recent issues of the magazine have both chronicled America's misdeeds and affirmed our commitment to do better.

Issues penned by Christian writer Chuck Austen were particularly interesting to read in this regard. After confronting a Native American terrorist who tells Cap that every citizen is complicit in America's misdeeds, Cap concludes one issue with a monologue worth reprinting at length because it represents not only what Captain America stands for today, but what we may hope to recognize and reconcile for ourselves as Americans:

> I remember a time when it was easy to feel pride in the country. . . . When "this" country was my country right or wrong—and most of the time it was right. But times have changed, haven't they? The battles are less clear, the wars less noble—the cause less right—even in the shadow of 9–11. Dark men with a "cause" come at us like thieves in the night. . . . Men who consider their cause "noble." Men who consider their cause "holy." . . . This government can be wrong. Our politics can be flawed. We are, after all, a complex system run by human beings. But the country is good, and though it's no longer easy—I still feel pride in her. I still love her and I will fight to the death to protect her and keep her safe—so others can—as I know they will—make her right again—most of the time.[16]

Recently, in a major company-wide event drawn closely from conditions in post-9/11 America, Marvel Comics featured Captain America as the leader of one band of heroes in its "Civil War" story line. In that story, the Superhero Registration Act that Captain America and his followers opposed was a clear metaphor for the civil liberties given up under the Patriot Act, and in this and many respects, "Civil War" was a tremendously topical series that dealt with "civil liberties and national security, public safety and private freedom." Marvel writer Paul Jenkins told the audience of "Talk of the Nation" on National Public Radio that these stories were based on contemporary issues like wiretapping and surveillance done without the American public's knowledge and without judicial oversight, and said the stories asked how we decide whether individual freedoms should be jettisoned in hopes of making people safer.[17] Some were surprised that Cap willingly defied the law for what he believed, but this was in line with the character's actions after Watergate. Steve Englehart, his writer back in those days, explained that Captain America should be more than just a jingoistic or legalistic hero, that he should represent the best of America, "American principles rather than American government."[18] (Or to put it in bumper sticker philosophy that Americans of every political stripe can appreciate, "I don't have to like my president to love my country.")

After violent confrontations with the pro-Registration forces headed by Cap's friend Iron Man, Captain America surrendered, not because he had changed his mind about the registration of all heroes, but because he saw the damage the civil war was doing to the nation he loved. And he paid for it with his life; after being taken into custody, Captain America was assassinated in police custody on the way to his arraignment hearing.

This civil war, like the American War between the States in the nineteenth century, was a war that affected the lives of patriots on both sides and split families down the middle—even Marvel's First Family: the Fantastic Four. Reed Richards (Mr. Fantastic) puts his genius to work for the pro-registration side, spearheading the movement with Tony Stark (Iron Man) and Hank Pym, and helping to imprison those heroes who oppose the Registration Act in a sort of super-Guantanamo, a secret prison in the Negative Zone.

For Reed's wife, Sue, this is all too much, and at last she leaves Reed—and the Fantastic Four—to fight against the Registration Act alongside Captain America. But before she goes, she sums up her objections by telling Reed, "Sometimes the law is wrong. Sometimes the government is wrong. When that happens, you have to speak out. Even if you're alone. Especially if you're alone. . . . What are the rights and freedoms we say we cherish worth? Because I think they're worth dying for if necessary."[19]

We've seen how comics appropriate many of our mono-myths, including the archetypal savior/messiah story. Another powerful biblical monomyth used by comics is the Akedah, the Binding of Isaac, and it's particularly pertinent to any discussion about authority. That story, related in the book of Genesis, begins in this fashion:

After these things God tested Abraham. He said to him, "Abraham!" And he said, "Here I am."

He said, "Take your son, your only son Isaac, whom you love, and go to the land of Moriah, and offer him there as a burnt-offering on one of the mountains that I shall show you."

So Abraham rose early in the morning, saddled his donkey, and took two of his young men with him, and his son Isaac; he cut the wood for the burnt-offering, and set out and went to the place in the distance that God had shown him.

On the third day Abraham looked up and saw the place far away.

Then Abraham said to his young men, "Stay here with the donkey; the boy and I will go over there; we will worship, and then we will come back to you."

Abraham took the wood of the burnt-offering and laid it on his son Isaac, and he himself carried the fire and the knife. So the two of them walked on together.

Isaac said to his father Abraham, "Father!" And he said, "Here I am, my son." He said, "The fire and the wood are here, but where is the lamb for a burnt-offering?"

Abraham said, "God himself will provide the lamb for a burnt-offering, my son." So the two of them walked on together.

When they came to the place that God had shown him, Abraham built an altar there and laid the wood in order. He bound his son Isaac, and laid him on the altar, on top of the wood.

Then Abraham reached out his hand and took the knife to kill his son.[20]

The Akedah is a central text for Jews, Christians, and Muslims alike (Muslims believe that the story refers to their ancestor Ishmael, not to Abraham's other son, Isaac). The Binding story records the faithfulness of Abraham; for some Christian interpreters it has prefigured God's offering of Jesus. But although this central narrative is not mentioned in the rest of the Hebrew Bible, centuries of later Jewish interpretation and midrash (retellings of a Bible narrative to discover essential truths) uncover another powerful layer of mythic meaning. First, although artistic interpretations of the scene have often depicted Isaac as a child, the narrative suggests at least a robust youth, since it is Isaac who carries the wood for his own sacrifice; interpreters from Josephus to the Talmud propose that Isaac is in his twenties or thirties. In any case, at the time of this story, Isaac's father, Abraham, is a man well over one hundred, and Isaac, in this understanding, is either a youth or a strong man who could, if he wished, certainly prevent his ancient father from binding him.

The Akedah is, in these Jewish interpretations, at least as much about the faith of Isaac as the faith of Abraham. Whether this faith is in God or in his father, Isaac trusts that someone in a position of authority, someone other than himself, knows better than he does what should transpire, and so he willingly acquiesces, even to the point of his sacrificial death. Bruce Feiler has noted that one of the ideas enthroned in the Akedah story is "our willingness to trust our fathers."[21] For this reason, the Binding of Isaac represents a supremely conservative myth that suggests that father always knows best, that the young must wait their turn and bide their time, doing the bidding of their fathers even if perhaps they do not understand it.[22] The Akedah remains a central monomyth explaining the workings of American society, albeit one that comics have reinterpreted as time has passed and circumstances have changed.

In the golden age of comics, with many of the mythically resonant characters like Superman, Batman, Wonder Woman, and Captain America who have entered American culture, we initially find simplistic and often extremely conservative applications of the Binding. As the American monomyth suggests, the traditional comics narrative is essentially conservative; the hero or heroine typically emerges to deal only with symptoms, not with root causes of crime, hatred, or injustice. Batman, for example, is forever dealing with escapees from the revolving door that is Arkham Asylum, that pathetically inadequate institution used to lock up his foes. And so Batman beats up the Joker/the Riddler/ the Penguin and so on by the end of the comic, and the villain or villains are led away in chains or we see them ensconced behind prison bars. But Batman doesn't ever ask why Arkham Asylum is so porous, let alone why there are so many criminals and dangerous lunatics on the streets of Gotham City. Such systemic questions would not even have occurred to the character, his creators, or to his readers until the 1960s or later.

This conservative pattern began to be altered in the 1960s and 1970s as Marvel and DC Comics told increasingly relevant stories about social issues (one remembers the famous query from a poor African American to DC characters Green Lantern and Green Arrow about why they helped multicolored aliens but not people of color here at home), and the 1980s brought a sharp break with heroic tradition. Although this change is sometimes described in literary or cultural terms as the development of more nuanced heroes or even of antiheroes, it also represents a sharp alteration in the understanding of the Binding. The major 1980s works questioning the fitness of the Akedah are *Watchmen* (the title is drawn from Juvenal's "Who watches the watchmen?") and Frank Miller's *Dark Knight Returns*. The moral complexity and ambiguity often noted in these comics that went on to change the industry actually results from a rejection of the Akedah as an appropriate myth with which to order American life.

This rejection of a "Father knows best" society had been played out elsewhere in American popular culture (films of the late 1960s such as *The Graduate* and *Bonnie and Clyde* had already begun to reach this conclusion; perhaps, freed as they were from a ratings code such as comics continued to labor under, they could more easily question authority), but nowhere is it more clearly stated than in *Dark Knight Returns* in the conflicts between the characters of Superman and Batman.

Superman has always been identified as an essentially conservative hero, often depicted with an American flag and represented as a defender of traditional values. The scene at the end of *Superman II* where Superman replaces the flag on top of the White House is perhaps *the* iconic example of his conformity to the status quo; although Superman has the power to change the world, he is content to let the occupant of the Oval Office make the important decisions while he cleans up the occasional mess. Superman and Batman meet early in *Dark Knight Returns*, after Batman in late middle age has decided to resume his career in a way that addresses what is wrong with society, not just what is wrong with its criminal element. In this meeting, Clark Kent/Superman tells Bruce Wayne/Batman, "Sooner or later, somebody's going to order me to bring you in. Somebody with authority."[23] And although Bruce has pointed out earlier that no one can make Superman do anything he doesn't choose to do, Superman is willing to defer to the paternal "authority."

Batman sums it up later, during his epic battle with Superman in the streets of Gotham City:

You've always known just what to say.
"Yes"—you always say yes—to anyone with a badge—or a flag.[24]

This rejection of the Akedah as a binding metanarrative— this refusal to "put the flag back on top of the White House"— flavors many of the most significant comics to emerge in the twenty years since. The characters in the revisionist 1990s superhero title *The Authority* rejected outright the notion that those with strength and vitality should simply do the bidding of their elders; they themselves became the authorities making ethical and political decisions. *The Ultimates*, a contemporary retelling (a midrash, one might even say) of Marvel's Avengers, uses the backdrop of superhero conflict to question the second Iraq War and America's adopted role as the world's policeman, again presenting a story where the wisdom of the elders is questioned. And most recently, the Marvel Comics "Civil War" story line has shown how an iconic conservative character, Captain America, becomes an outlaw rather than obey a registration law he believes will stifle American freedom.

When Captain America begins to rebel against the government, then pretty clearly we are seeing the revision of this myth achieve widespread validity.

Unquestioning acceptance of a truth—any truth—is dangerous. And yet, we're sometimes told that to criticize the institutions we love is treasonous, an act of extreme disloyalty. America, right or wrong, love it or leave it. Captain America loved America enough to question it—and, in the tradition of peaceful protest in America, truly honored its laws by taking responsibility for his opposition. The Hebrew prophets often tried to amend the ways of the erring children of Israel. Martin Luther King Jr. often lovingly took the Christian church and the American nation to task for not being everything they could be. And Robert F. Kennedy—brother of an assassinated president, himself to fall before an assassin's bullet—spoke often about the right—and responsibility—of Americans to dissent. He once said,

> Democracy is no easy form of government. Few nations have been able to sustain it. For it requires that we take the chances of freedom; that the liberating play of reason be brought to bear on events filled with passion; that dissent be allowed to make its appeal for acceptance; that men chance error in their search for truth."[25]

And justice, we might add. And the American way.

The Problem of Evil

I'm not bad. I'm just drawn that way.
                    —From *Who Framed Roger Rabbit?*

Gotham City is a bad place. It may not be quite as bad as a few other locales in the world of comics—Darkseid's dark planet Apokolips, Dr. Doom's Latveria—but it's always been the comic book embodiment of a place of evil and chaos. In Frank Miller's *Batman: Year One*, future police commissioner James Gordon is shown arriving in town aboard a crowded train that looks like it belongs in a third-world country. "Gotham City," he muses to himself. "Maybe it's all I deserve, now. Maybe it's just my time in Hell."[1]

Gotham City is every nightmare vision of every great urban area ever created, and whether we talk about the cinematic Gotham created by production designer Anton Furst for Tim Burton's 1989 *Batman* or the dark Victorian/Art Deco monstrosity that resides in comics, we're talking about a city rife for—and seemingly designed for—crime, corruption, depravity. Planetary's sardonic old man Elijah Snow steps off a helicopter and onto a roof in Gotham, and gives its brief history: "Old as New York, founded on the East Coast and originally designed by English masons on opium . . . exacerbated by absinthe-fiend local architects in the twenties, basically not fit for human habitation . . . Gotham City."[2]

What makes some place so evil—or, rather, so filled with evil people? Is it the design, the architecture, the lack of light and air? Is it the economic and social conditions the city dwellers live under? Is it a lack of moral leadership?

Gotham City has had the Batman cleaning up the streets since 1939, and they aren't clean yet. What is it going to take to get rid of evil if Batman can't get the job done?

The nature of evil and origin of suffering has concerned practitioners of religion, philosophy, and the arts for millennia. Early ethical systems attempted to teach people to do what was right—which often meant, what was pleasing to the gods—and to avoid that which was wrong. When the Hebrews developed ethical monotheism, the role and origin of moral evil became more important. In early Hebrew thought, evil was held to be a given, a natural part of the universe. The Hebrew words for moral evil and calamity are all but identical, and evil was "anything that is unpleasant, repulsive, or distorted."[3]

But thinking of evil as a necessary part of the universe brings up all sorts of philosophical and theological questions, especially for people of faith. If, as many people believe, a benevolent force created the universe, then why was evil made a part of it? And to what extent is that force involved with the presence of evil? The story of Job, in the Hebrew Bible, presents the question in a debate, first between Job and his friends as to why such calamity has befallen Job, and then at last, in a dialogue between Job and God.

The final lesson from Job isn't particularly satisfying to our human need to understand; God tells Job, essentially, "That's just the way things are, okay? Stop asking such questions." But we can't stop. The questions are among the things that make us human, and Peter J. Gomes, the pastor to the Harvard University community, wrestles with them anew in his book about reading the Bible today, *The Good Book*. He examines three troubling scenarios: God is indifferent (and if this is true, who wants to serve such a God?); God is sympathetic but powerless (again, how is this helpful to us in our day-to-day lives?); God is the Source or cause of suffering (and really, what kind of God would this be? Not one anybody would want to worship, that's for sure).[4] So Gomes looks past the question of God's involvement to the question of suffering's purpose: "God's role," he tells us, is not to relieve suffering or to spare us from it, but to enable us to bear it and endure it so that even our suffering is redemptive for ourselves and others."[5] Suffering, then, is a part of human experience, and it has a redemptive purpose.

All the same, we want to know where evil comes from, and we like to put a face on it, particularly when it's a face that doesn't look like ours. In comics, we make the villains grotesque, like the Joker or the Red Skull; we make them obviously beyond the pale so we can distance ourselves from them and their actions. In the early Christian church, this was largely done through the personification of evil in the character of Satan and Satan's "assignment" as ruler of this fallen world. Again, it's an enticing idea. Chris Seay and I summarize this view in *The Gospel Reloaded*: "Why do bad things happen to good people? . . . Satan caused them. Why do good people do bad things? Satan tempted them. When is the world going to be a better place? When Satan gets thrown out of it."[6] Giving a supernatural character like Satan so much power takes us off the hook to a certain extent, and gives us explanations for the way the world is.

But frankly, telling ourselves such a story can also be a mammoth cop-out. Because as Gomes tells us in his chapter on evil, he'd like to write a book and call it *Why Good People Do Bad Things*, since he meets so many people who want to know why they do things that hurt others, why they carry around horrible thoughts in their hearts and heads, why they do things they know they shouldn't. "The Bible," he reminds us, "is filled with vivid images of people caught between the knowledge of what is good and what is evil, and the inability to avoid the easy wrong and affirm the difficult right."[7] To say, with comedian Flip Wilson, that "the devil made me do it" is to avoid our own responsibility—and our own knowledge—that each of us is capable of things we would rather not do.

In the 2002 DC Comics graphic novel *JLA/JSA: Virtue and Vice*, the Seven Deadly Sins, which were formerly all caged up in the cave of the ancient wizard Shazam, get turned loose to infect members of the Justice League and the Justice Society. It would seem like a case of "the devil made me do it," except for one thing: In almost every one of these "possessions," it's easy to see that the Sins are simply magnified versions of the character's already-existing behavior. Take Batman, for example: in the grip of Anger, he urges Gotham City citizens to form lynch mobs and take back the streets. But it's really only a step beyond his own behavior as Dark Knight, Gotham's vigilante prompted by his own anger over his parents' deaths. Or Power Girl, who is hyped up by the spirit of Lust: Even in a world of overripe heroines and comic cleavage, how many teenage boys over the years have wondered how she keeps from falling out of that costume? And the latest Green Lantern, Kyle Raynor, egged on by Envy? Kyle has spent his young career as a superhero surrounded by people who remember past Lanterns (and, in *Virtue and Vice*, he's in the company of Guardian, the original Golden Age Green Lantern); just a slight magnification of Kyle's own insecurity makes him into a monster.

Here is one of the hard truths about sin and evil; while we like to ascribe a source of evil out there somewhere, the fact is, we are all sources of it. It's why in the Jewish and Muslim traditions believers are enjoined to act with justice, why in the Christian tradition many followers confess their sins and pledge to amend their ways, why in the Buddhist tradition people are urged to meditate on the suffering of the world and to try not to add to that suffering.

It would be lovely if evil wore a garish costume and cackled a horrible laugh. But evil can look like each and every one of us. One of the most compelling elements of Max Allan Collins's graphic novel *Road to Perdition* is the character of Michael O'Sullivan, the gangster enforcer known as the Angel of Death. A soldier who survived the First World War and who tells his son he kills for a living because being a soldier is the only thing he knows, he's also the man his son describes in this way: "He was quiet, my father, and the most honorable man I ever knew. He was what they used to call a family man. He didn't drink. He didn't whore. Maybe you think he did and just didn't tell me . . . but I know he didn't."[8]

Moreover, Michael is a deeply religious man; after every gangland killing, even when he and his son are on the run from Al Capone and his gang, he stops in a Catholic church, lights a candle for the men he has killed, and confesses his sins to a priest. Later, after his son, Michael Jr., asks him, "Am I a sinner, Papa?" he replies, "We're all sinners, son. That's the way we enter this world. But we can leave it forgiven."[9]

Comics are full of sinful beings, people who have many good qualities yet who do evil, just as the world is full of them. The act of taking the law into your own hands, as we'll see in the next chapter, can force even heroes to carry out rough justice, and if something as basic to our understanding of comic heroes can be so morally ambiguous, you can guess that lots of other heroes have erred in more meaningful ways. From Hank Pym/Giant-Man beating his wife to Avenger Carol Danvers showing up for work drunk to Green Lantern committing cosmic catastrophe under the influence of the villain Parallax to heroes on both sides of Marvel's "Civil War" teaming up with supervillains who happen to support their position on the Superhero Registration Act, plenty of our heroes have perpetrated evil.

And, as we'll see, sometimes we don't even have to act to create negative consequences. Sometimes doing nothing is as bad as doing something wrong. In the Anglican prayer book, the prayer of confession speaks of both those things we ought not to have done and those things we ought to have done. That is, both action and inaction can be sources of evil.

So let's begin with personal evil, of which there are ample examples in comics. When we look at those seven deadly sins we can find a number of familiar faces: pride, lust, gluttony, anger, sloth, envy, and greed have prompted plenty of villains, fictional and real. (These sins are not biblical, by the way, although they've taken on the stamp of authenticity because they ring true to our experience.)

Pride, for example, is one of the engines driving villains like Dr. Doom and Magneto and Lex Luthor: I'm the smartest, I'm the best, I ought to be in charge. But it also snares heroes; one of Spider-Man's great temptations in *Spider-Man 3* is pride. As director Sam Raimi told film writers,

> Peter considers himself a sinless person compared to these villains. . . . We felt it would be great for him to learn a less black-and-white view of life—that he's not above these people, that he's not just the hero, that they're not just the villains, but we're all human beings. He had to learn that he himself might have some sin within him, and that other human beings—the ones he calls the criminals—have humanity within them. And that the best we can do in this world is to not strive for vengeance, but for forgiveness.[10]

Personal evil is a result of giving in to these negative impulses to pursue our own self-satisfaction at the expense of others. It may seem pleasant at the time; it may even seem to make us happy. But, as Thomas Merton tells us, such selfishness "always leads to sorrow because it narrows and deadens our spirit."[11] Every faith tradition tells us that unselfishness and compassion and love are the answers; the Dalai Lama goes so far as to tell us that even if we rejected all religion and ideology, we still "cannot escape the necessity of love and compassion," which is at the heart of those traditions.[12]

So why do so many of us still have trouble doing the right thing?

Part of the problem may also come because of the way we're raised and socialized. Since evil is a part of us as individuals, it can also be a part of the systems we create and the institutions of which we're a part. Societal evil—what Gomes insightfully calls "sins of the system"—can come in the forms of racism and other prejudice, militarism, sexism, unbridled capitalism, and other ailments, but the end result of all of this is two things: a system that damages the people inside the society holding these beliefs and damages the people against whom these beliefs are held.

The world abounds, unfortunately, in examples of nations that have damaged themselves through their societal sins. Perhaps the best example in our own history is in the ongoing battle for civil rights. Martin Luther King Jr. spent a great deal of time in his essay "Letter from Birmingham Jail" discussing why racism was harmful to all of American society, and in one of the most telling lines from that document, he took to task not just the violent extremists who burned crosses and killed his black brothers and sisters, but everyone who participated in the sins by continuing as a part of the system: "We will have to repent in this generation not merely for the vitriolic words and actions of the bad people, but for the appalling silence of the good people."[13]

The victims of this sort of societal abuse often fight back in the only ways they can. Sometimes they fight violence with violence, anger with anger, as the Black Panthers did in the 1960s or as the Palestinians do in Israel today. Sometimes their psyches are scarred by the repression and pain. A textbook example of a societal victim in comics is Alan Moore's Joker in *The Killing Joke*.

One of the few truly convincing origin stories for one of comics' greatest villains, *The Killing Joke* posits an out-of-work (and not very good) comedian trying to feed his family who gets caught up in a criminal scheme and ultimately loses his family, his good name, his identity, and his sanity because of it. What kind of society forces such choices on people—crime or starvation? Only one that has posited that all who are worth saving will save themselves. (The Penguin, in Tim Burton's film *Batman Returns*, shows another example of a victim who becomes a villain; rejected by the world above and sent into the sewers, Burton's Penguin is a pathetic and angry creation who simply wants revenge on the world that threw him away.)

Of course, the notion of social evil nudges us into so many gray areas it can seem almost impossible for us to proceed. In many interpretations of his character, for example, the Joker is insane or a sociopath; many other comic villains seem to be either unable to distinguish right from wrong or unable to care about the difference. When circumstances—a person's life, society's treatment, or other factors—create such a character who does evil, what should our response be?

And to complicate things even further, when people do acts of great evil—the mass murders at Columbine High School or at Virginia Tech, for example—many psychiatrists would tell us that this behavior is a textbook example of sociopathy, the actions of someone who lacks a social conscience. Yet the evil is no less potent, the victims no less dead, because it is done by someone without a concept of how great an evil it is. When Bizarro, Superman's strange shadow, acts violently, who should be held responsible? In Alan Moore's *Superman: Whatever Happened to the Man of Tomorrow*, when Bizarro kills everyone on his planet, then himself, the end result can only be some befuddled head shaking.

We can also see one last element of the role of evil in comic books. If evil is a necessary part of the divine plan, then is evil itself in service of the divine plan? Writers and theologians alike have suggested that, of course. The apostle Paul spoke of how all things work for good; Augustine wrote that after a lengthy bout of rumination on God and the problem of evil, it became "clear to me that you [God] made all things good, and there are absolutely no substances which you did not make."[14] The English poet John Milton wrote his epic poem "Paradise Lost" in part to justify the ways of God to human beings, to show how the storied fall of Adam and Eve was a fortunate one leading to the great miracle of incarnation and personal salvation in the birth and sacrifice of Jesus. The philosopher Friedrich Nietzsche even argued that behavior most of us would label immoral or evil—injustice, cruelty, and selfishness—was necessary to create and preserve human civilization (it was while examining this "will to power," incidentally—which Nietzsche said allows the more gifted, intelligent, and strong of humans to create a culture on the backs of lesser beings—that he first coined the term "superman").[15] So paradoxically, evil seems to somehow be an essential part of the system.

The character of Galactus in Marvel Comics dramatically demonstrates this paradox. One of the most powerful of antagonists, he has often menaced Earth, and on many occasions, has destroyed worlds populated by billions of sentient beings to consume their energies. Compared to the Joker or Green Goblin or Kingpin or even big-time bad guys like the Red Skull, Dr. Doom, and Magneto, Galactus tops all the most-wanted lists. Yet, in an epic story line in *Fantastic Four* in the early 1980s, it became clear that Galactus—mass murderer on a cosmic scale—was nothing more or less than a force of nature. Artist and writer John Byrne depicted Galactus in a scene with the goddess Death (the embodiment of death in the Marvel Universe and the sometime motivation of another cosmic bad guy, Thanos, to destroy the universe in her honor); during this scene, Death suggests on several occasions that Galactus serves a vital purpose. "The universe is young," she says, "and you have much to do," and she later tells him, "Yours is quite possibly the most important role. Do not shirk it, lest the universe fail at the last."[16]

Later in the story line, Galactus is put on trial by the vast Shi'ar empire for his crimes against life in the universe, and in one of the strangest courtroom dramas in literature, cosmic truth is revealed to all in the proceeding room. This sort of transcendent transfer of ultimate knowledge is denied to us, the comics readers, however, so I will reproduce the most potent evidence, the testimony of the Fantastic Four's resident genius, Reed Richards:

> When Galactus came to Earth all those long years ago we were told by the Watcher that he was not evil—that Galactus is in fact beyond good and evil. . . . Albert Einstein once said that "God does not play at dice." He meant that there is an order of things in our universe. And it does not require any belief in a supreme being to realize that Galactus must somehow be part of that order—and, I suspect, an important part. For if he is truly to be considered neutral, then the apparent evil of his actions must, in the end result, not be evil. And so, they must be part of some greater good. . . . Ultimately I have no proof. . . . I have only logic . . . logic and faith.[17]

Galactus proved to be a part of the greater plan, however unknowable that plan might be to us. (It's similar to the way Gandalf in *The Fellowship of the Ring* tells Frodo Baggins that the villainous Gollum has some essential part in the working out of Middle-earth's salvation, which also proves to be true.) I'm reminded of these stories when I think of the character we call Satan. In the Hebrew Bible, Satan is God's tester in the book of Job; perhaps evil and calamity are the ultimate tests for all of us. Will we choose to do right? Will we succumb to despair? Will we follow the path of evil ourselves? If these tests help us become better people, stronger in faith, more determined to do good instead of evil, isn't it possible that even Satan serves a vital function in God's universe?

Ultimately, we face the same problems that our superheroes face. There are bad people in the world whose actions and ideas must be overcome; there are evil systems in the world that must be overthrown. And there are our own evil impulses that must be overwhelmed before they can overwhelm us.

We are all going to be creatures who combine good and evil; none of us is perfect. But every faith tradition encourages us to be more mindful of what good and evil really are, to more totally integrate our beliefs and our actions. We may never wrestle a villain more powerful than one of our siblings, but we can wrestle with evil just as heroically as any character we've ever admired.

Vigilante Justice

I'm the best there is at what I do. Only what I do isn't very nice.
—Wolverine

As we saw earlier in the book, comic superheroes—from the great icons like Superman, Batman, Spider-Man, and Captain America all the way down—all operate in the strange territory some have called "pop fascism"—the realm in which super-powered beings with a clearly developed sense of what justice ought to be step forward and take action when other entities won't. However well intentioned they may be, most of our comic heroes are what we would call "vigilantes," people who work outside the normal channels of law to administer justice.

Americans weren't the first vigilantes; although one of government's primary functions is to provide protection and justice, people throughout history have taken the law into their own hands when they felt that the system had failed them. The Jewish religious leaders who detained Jesus and brought him before the Roman authority Pontius Pilate were, they thought, serving justice (and, conveniently, removing one of the chief threats to themselves and their position in society). The popular revolts of the fourteenth century—the Jacquerie in France and the Peasants' Revolt in England—grew out of the common people's sense of injustice, their lack of legal and political rights, their oppression by the rich and powerful. One of the most important popular culture renderings of an uprising against injustice—and one of the most important tales of vigilante justice—can be found in the stories of Robin Hood, who redistributes wealth as he distributes justice in Sherwood Forest. Like many comic characters, he's a hero and an outlaw at the same time.

But although we find examples throughout world history, vigilantism seems to fit particularly well into the American psyche; the word "vigilante" first came into usage in English in America in the mid-nineteenth century to describe "a member of a self-appointed group of citizens who undertake law enforcement in their community without legal authority, typically because the legal agencies are thought to be inadequate."[1] Members of these so-called vigilance committees served as self-appointed police officers, judges, and—sometimes—executioners. Nineteenth-century author and politician Stephen Palfrey Webb wrote a sketch of the Vigilance Committee formed in 1856 in wild and woolly San Francisco, California, and included in his work the constitution ratified by that group. It could stand in for many of the oaths taken by caped wonders and reflects the philosophies espoused by most of the crime fighters to be found in comics:

> The citizens whose names are hereunto attached, do unite themselves into an association for maintenance of the peace and good order of society; the prevention and punishment of crime; the preservation of our lives and property; and to insure that our ballot boxes shall hereafter express the actual and unforged will of the majority of our citizens; and we do bind ourselves each to the other by a solemn oath to do and perform every just and lawful act for the maintenance of law and order, and to sustain the laws when properly and faithfully administered. But we are determined that no thief, burglar, incendiary, assassin, ballot box stuffer, or other disturber of the peace shall escape punishment, either by the quibbles of the law, the insecurity of prisons, the carelessness or corruption of the police, or the laxity of those who pretend to administer justice.[2]

It might remind us of the oath taken by Green Lantern: "By brightest day and darkest night, no evil shall escape my sight. Let those who worship evil's might, beware my power—Green Lantern's light!"

Since through much of our history people living at the edges of American civilization were largely responsible for their own safety and for keeping the peace, many of our literary and culture heroes are people who have taken the law into their own hands, made their own decisions on ultimate right and wrong. Hawkeye/Natty Bumppo/Leatherstocking (the many-named hero of James Fenimore Cooper's "Leatherstocking Tales," including *The Last of the Mohicans*) was the first of many frontier heroes who administered justice based on their own code; Western heroes, beginning with the hero of Owen Wister's *The Virginian* and extending to the Lone Ranger and beyond, administered their own brand of frontier justice in the absence of courts and police officers; and in contemporary settings where law and order don't hold sway and gangs or mob violence are active, we see action heroes—particularly the kind of characters played by Arnold Schwarzenegger, Sylvester Stallone, and Bruce Willis—taking matters into their own hands with lots of firepower and catchy sayings.

Likewise, in comics, plenty of characters have some sort of official mandate. The Avengers at one time held a charter from the United Nations; Captain Atom served President Lex Luthor; Superman is a quasi-official superhero in the Dark Knight stories of Frank Miller; Stormwatch, Top-10, and the superpowered FBI agents in *Powers* are working within the system, as are those Marvel heroes who have signed the Superhero Registration Act and become members of the so-called Initiative. But most of the heroes we read about do not. They're doing the same thing as Robin Hood—distributing justice where it isn't, perhaps helping out the forces of law and order, but not working within the same confines, rules, and regulations.

The word "vigilante" comes from the root word "awake," and it implies someone looking out for others. But in American vigilante justice, the truth of the matter is that justice is rarely selfless;

as John Shelton Lawrence and Robert Jewett observe in their discussion of the Lone Ranger as part of the vigilante hero archetype, "extralegal violence and personal vengeance" are both essential to the story.[3] American heroes are often forced into action by circumstances, just as Americans like to think that America only involves itself in violence overseas when it has no other choice. The Lone Ranger initially puts on his mask to avenge the death of his fellow Texas Rangers (ever wonder why he's the *Lone* Ranger?); Bruce Willis's character in *Die Hard* takes on the bad guys because they're threatening his wife; Arnold Schwarzenegger's character in *Commando* opens up a can of butt-kicking on the bad guys who have kidnapped his daughter; and so on.

Revenge as justice.

This idea of personal justice extends into the world of comics. Batman's entire existence is a result of his personal quest for justice. The very name of the Avengers, the marquee super group of Marvel Comics, suggests their modus operandi: attack us, and we'll hit you back harder. It's a very American way to respond. As author and *Time* magazine political columnist Joe Klein has noted, "The American Way of war seems—unfortunately, or maybe not—to be a full-blooded, lethal response only after the country has been taken by surprise."[4]

And therein lies the last of the major elements of the American vigilante idea: to achieve justice, the vigilante must meet violence with overwhelming force, whether the large numbers of a Vigilance Committee turning out to round up (and possibly lynch) a supposed evildoer, the incredible marksmanship and speed of the Lone Ranger, the big guns of Schwarzenegger's character in almost any movie, or the finely developed or superhuman powers of our heroes in comics. Thus the philosophical argument about what is right is answered as it was in the Arthurian legends, before the coming of the Round Table: Might makes right. As Lawrence and Jewett point out, these stories reinforce the idea that "All one needs to escape the ambiguity of violent power is more power. . . . The vigilante has become the saint, not merely though superior virtue but also because of superhuman power."[5]

And here's where things become morally troubling. With some characters in comics, the moral code is absolute: Superman doesn't kill, ever; Green Arrow, as recounted in Kevin Smith's story arc "Quiver," falls into despair when he breaks this rule. The common argument against lethal force, expressed in comics for decades, typically boils down to this: If we use their methods, then we're no better than them. The practical argument, outside the frame of the story, is that the Comics Code calls for comic books appearing under its imprimatur to somehow reconcile the following requirements: "In every instance good shall triumph over evil and the criminal [be] punished for his misdeeds; . . . scenes of excessive violence shall be prohibited."[6]

And so when a character does kill, as the Warbird character did in an issue of *Avengers*, or use excessive force, which is the common complaint about characters like the Huntress, the Punisher, or Wolverine, it's often a matter of some consternation to the rest of the heroic community. Comics, at least typically, pay lip service to the idea that justice must be achieved with a minimum of brutality, that to indulge in this superviolence is indeed to descend to the level of the foe. In the early days of the New X-Men, group leaders Cyclops and Storm both clashed with Wolverine to try and rein him in; bruising, broken bones, maybe even maiming were okay in the pursuit of punishing criminals for their misdeeds.

But outright murder was not.

In this respect, comics were reflecting Jewish tenets on justice, as well as the tenets of Christianity (and other faith traditions) rejecting violence as a solution. In Jewish law, retribution and justice were not permitted to exceed what was necessary to impose punishment. One of the most controversial passages from the Hebrew Bible comes from the book of Exodus, where God gives Moses a set of laws about justice. "An eye for an eye," which we find in the twenty-first chapter of Exodus, symbolizes for modern people a sort of brutal and barbaric standard, but really, these passages do more than just mandate punishment; they also, as Rabbi Joseph Telushkin points out, limit it to what is right and decent, unlike some other codes of justice in the ancient world. (Exodus, for example, does not endorse the taking of two eyes for an eye, while records from early Jewish proceedings indicate that offenders responsible for someone's blindness were not blinded themselves, but were instead forced to pay compensation.) The point of this biblical code was ultimately the same as the Comics Code: "Evil must be punished, and punishment must be proportionate to, and not exceed, the offense."[7] To do more than that is to create the possibility of an unjust justice.

That's why even some of comics' most iconic characters begin to cause us problems as we examine them. Take Batman, for example, the fearsome Dark Knight Detective. His approach—instilling fear in the underworld through his appearance and his willingness to do violence—has always caused problems with the sunnier, less morally ambiguous superheroes who assume the high moral ground, notably Superman. For them, whatever his good results, Batman goes about the job the wrong way.

Since his creation, Superman has been the noblest embodiment of right, fueled not by a personal quest for revenge but by the responsibility to use his powers for the greater good. Scottish comics writer Grant Morrison does a fine job of summarizing both Superman's importance and his uniqueness as a purveyor of American extrajudicial justice:

> After years of cowboys, soldiers, tough private eyes and gangsters at a time in the late 1930s when America's self-image was built around the use of guns as means to tame a young and restless country . . . [Jerry Siegel and Joe Shuster] came up with their brilliant notion: an All-American icon hero with a code against killing. Here we have a living flag, who always uses his immense strength and super-intelligence to solve problems without leaving a trail of bodies in his wake. What a forward thinking, utopian idea that is! Superman as the new world testament![8]

Early in the *Superman/Batman* comic, writer Jeph Loeb dramatically reveals—in parallel panels on the same page—the contrast between the two heroes. On the left, the Superman panel, bathed in light: "My parents taught me to side with justice. . . . I'm known as a hero, an inspiration, a champion. It's been a good life." On the right, the Batman panel, showing Batman's face cloaked in darkness: "My parent's killer was never brought to justice. . . . I'm known as an urban myth, a frightening creature, the bogeyman. It is not a life I would wish on anyone."[9]

If Superman represents the light and reason, the positive possibilities of extralegal justice, Batman is the dark side. Even though he has devoted his life to justice, there's something that seems just the slightest bit—unhealthy? unwholesome?—about the whole thing. Frank Miller captures the tensions expertly in *The Dark Night Returns* by showing dozens of viewpoints on the Batman: many people think Batman is a frightening rogue who drags justice through the gutter. Likewise in the popular Justice League of America graphic novel *The Nail*, penned by Alan Davis, Lois Lane tells Batman he is his own worst enemy: "You immerse yourself in mystery and superstition. . . . You deliberately scare people."[10] And he's not just frightening as an image of retribution; he's frightening in person. Batman has more than just a dark exterior; he has a dark side, a shadow that ties him to the villains he hates and hunts. It is the shadow fallen over Bruce Wayne even in *Batman Begins* that causes childhood friend and present-day love interest Rachel Dawes (Katie Holmes) to proclaim that the man she loved is gone: "*This* is your mask. Your real face is the one that criminals now fear. The man I loved—the man who vanished—he never came back at all."

Perhaps this fearsome side comes out most prominently in the wildly popular "Hush" story line penned by Jeph Loeb for *Batman*. In one of the most powerful—and moving—comics in recent memory, Batman is faced with the Joker—his oldest and cruelest foe, killer of the second Robin, of Commissioner Gordon's wife, Sarah, and just previous to the issue in question (he thinks), of Bruce Wayne's childhood friend Tommy Elliot.

That's it; game over. Batman finally concludes that the Joker deserves to die, then and there, at his hands.

So Batman beats the Joker unmercifully—the issue juxtaposes these brutal images with Batman's memories and justification for the death sentence he is imposing—and he gives the same treatment to his love interest, Catwoman, when she attempts to stop him. In fact Batman doesn't rein in the violence until Jim Gordon—the former police commissioner, and his closest friend—appeals to his reason, his highest instincts, his heroism.

"You and I have seen more than our fair share of tragedies and thirsted for revenge," Gordon says. "If Batman wanted to be a killer, he could have started a long time ago. But it's a line. On one side we believe in the law. On the other . . . sometimes the law fails us. Maybe that's why I've understood you . . . allowed you to help protect this city. Batman, if you cross that line—if you kill the Joker tonight—I will lead the hunt to bring you to justice. In the eyes of the law . . . in my eyes you'll be no different from him."[11]

At the end, Batman returns to his senses—and remembers which side of the line he belongs on. But not every contemporary comics hero knows—or cares.

Take the Punisher, Marvel's vigilante character and the hero of the 2004 movie starring Thomas Jane. Created in the early 1970s in the pages of *Spider-Man* by writer Gerry Conway, the Punisher was a gritty character who fit into the edgier revenge narratives emerging in popular culture like *Death Wish*, the 1974 Charles Bronson film that featured the ad slogan "Vigilante, city style—Judge, Jury, and Executioner." The Punisher was a Vietnam veteran whose family was killed by mobsters, and like Bruce Wayne, he was, frankly, pretty upset about it. But unlike Batman, from the beginning of his struggle to wipe out organized crime, the Punisher used knives, guns, and lethal force, and subsequently found himself even further on the other side of the law and public opinion than Batman.

The irony, of course, is that to most observers he is simply a criminal killing other criminals. At one point he is arrested, tried, and—to his great satisfaction—put in prison alongside other violent offenders. Nonetheless, the Punisher has become one of the most popular characters in Marvel Comics, appearing in his own books and crossing over into most of the other comics in the Marvel Universe. He also spawned a DC Comics copycat introduced in 1980—a former district attorney who took rough justice into his own hands using the nom de guerre of (what else?) Vigilante.

As comics began to publish for more diverse audiences, it was no longer necessary for all titles to meet the strict standards of the Comics Code, which prohibited graphic violence. *The Punisher* was one of the Marvel titles that benefited most from an adult ("Mature") treatment. The Punisher comics have had the freedom to become more brutal, more bloody, and more like the R-rated films that are their closest analogue. Revenge as justice as entertainment.

When the Punisher shows up in the books of other Marvel heroes—such as Spider-Man—the contrast of methods becomes most obvious. Just as with the working tension between Superman and Batman, most of the mainstream heroes of the Marvel Universe don't countenance killing, and often will try to keep the Punisher from exacting ultimate vengeance. In *Civil War*, Captain America beats him within an inch of his life for killing bad guys. The same tensions appear in Alan Moore's *Watchmen*, where the paranoid right-wing vigilante Rorshach, who uses the most brutal of methods to fight crime, is continually upbraided by his colleagues, who follow the classical comics approach: disarm and disable with a minimum of force. The contrast in methods is presented with chilling humor when characters remember a common antagonist, Captain Carnage, a small-time hood who actually got into villainy because he enjoyed being beat up: the Owl walked away from Captain Carnage as the villain pleaded to be punished; Rorshach dropped him down an elevator shaft.[12]

And while the story is funny, it's also a clear reminder of the morality of the matter; what Rorshach did was just plain wrong. It may be that for some characters, the ends justify any means, but for others, if you have to stop being a hero to accomplish your ends, then maybe they're not worth accomplishing.

And that's the way it should be; ultimately, however interesting we may find the violent heroes of the comics world (Wolverine, whom we'll discuss more in the next chapter, is among the most popular characters in comics history), the measure of a hero has to be more than just getting the job done, getting the bad guys off the street whichever way.

Like Superman, the heroes who provide the best example for us are the ones with an unshakable moral code, something we can aspire to. It's easy to think pragmatically; that's a particularly American trait. But doing what is right has to be more than just doing what works in a given situation, or morality doesn't really exist.

Seeing how superheroes deal with the kind of human problems we might face can be instructive. In issues of *Daredevil* written by Brian Michael Bendis, the character of Matt Murdock/ Daredevil has faced many problems that couldn't simply be solved by a well-placed fist, and his response to them has been morally ambiguous. Matt tells his friend and law partner Foggy Nelson that he misses going toe-to-toe with one of his most dangerous foes, Wilson Fisk/the Kingpin, because, he says, "I knew where I stood with Wilson, I knew the rules."[13]

Matt has turned to pragmatism instead of relying on a rock-solid moral code to do what's right. And as a result, one of Matt's friends, fellow superhero Luke Cage, tells him he's turned into a "lowlife piece of garbage." Luke goes on to explain: "Our entire existence, we put on the outfit—all the crap we been through— what puts us apart from the lowlifes is how we behaved with the crap we didn't ask for. . . . Be a man! Stand for something more than just a pair of tights."[14]

How do you do the right thing? Well, in the morally ambiguous world of vigilante justice that can be hard to say. But there's always the example of Superman, or Captain America, or any of a number of our comics heroes who do what they can to eliminate the specter of personal revenge from their pursuit of justice. At its core, might doesn't make right. It simply makes.

In one of his sermons, Martin Luther King Jr. noted that "violence brings only temporary victories; violence, by creating many more social problems than it solves, never brings permanent peace."[15] Although our popular culture often tells us otherwise, we really shouldn't admire anyone or anything just because it can shoot faster, punch harder, or see through walls, because it's the toughest or most powerful. Instead, we should admire those who do what's right—that's all that matters. As the Hebrew prophet Amos put it, "Seek good and not evil—and live!"[16]

It is often dramatically satisfying for us to watch the hero dismember, blow up, or smash the bad guy to a pulp in a movie, story, or comic. But some part of us knows the truth: what sets good apart from evil is that we're not really like that.

Or, at least, that we shouldn't be.

The Beast

The beast in me is caged by frail and fragile bars
Restless by day and by night . . .
God help the beast in me.
                    —Johnny Cash (from a song written
                            for him by Nick Lowe)

In 1976, one of the X-Men, Henry McCoy—you probably know him as the Beast—made a bad decision. Like Dr. Jekyll before him, he drank a potion that altered him in body, mind, and soul—that turned him from an agile adventurer with big feet into an actual beast. For a space in *Amazing Adventures* 11 (1972), the happy-go-lucky McCoy, once the X-Men's intellectual, was transformed into a raving, raging blue simian animal who had no control over his actions. Although he later recovered his sanity—his control—the story line is instructive for us in that it captures one of the central archetypes of good and evil: the beast or darkness within.

As we discussed briefly in "The Problem of Evil," we have different ideas of where evil comes from. Some of us are drawn, of course, to the idea of an external evil, Satan, for example, who tempts us to do wrong, tries to get us on its team. Others say that evil comes from inside us, grows out of our dark desires and weaknesses. Everyone has a secret place (or as Bruce Springsteen sang in "Darkness on the Edge of Town," everyone's got a secret they just can't face, and one day they let it drag them down).

And from that secret place, we see the things we don't want to do—the things we fear about ourselves—emerge.

In literature and popular culture we find plenty of examples of this sort of shadow, both as a different part of ourselves (Dr. Jekyll/Mr. Hyde) or as a reflection or doppelganger that reveals parts of us the mirror doesn't show (Dr. Faustus and the demon Mephistopheles, in the various versions of the Faustus legend). Anthony Stevens wrote that our fascination with these stories of inner—or reflected—evil are archetypal, attractive yet repellent at the same time, and the popularity of characters who exemplify these traits seems to bear that out. "The stories of Jekyll and Faust," he wrote, "like the Biblical story of Adam's fall, are cautionary tales that bring us down to earth and back to the eternal reality of our own evil."[1]

In comics, some of our most powerful archetypal characters are examples of these characters who carry the beast within, the shadow that must always be fought. Alan Moore's Mr. Hyde, from *League of Extraordinary Gentlemen*, of course, is the dark side of Dr. Jekyll—so extraordinarily evil and unrestrained that he can't hide. He grows to enormous size and commits the most hideous (another echo of that name?) of acts: blood-spattering violence, dismemberment, rape, murder.

In many Christian narratives, devils and demons are characters who come from without to tempt people to do evil. In the fourth chapter of the Gospel of Luke, Jesus is tempted by the devil to give up his mission before it even starts, and in the Gospel of John, it is the devil who tempts Judas to turn Jesus over to the authorities: "The Devil by now had Judas . . . firmly in his grip, all set for the betrayal."[2] But at other times in the Gospel narratives, demons and devils are already within people, and it's instructive to remember these stories in connection with the work of the existential psychologist Rollo May, who used the terms "demon" or "daimon" as a less supernatural explanation for evil: "The daimonic is any natural function which has the power to take over the whole person." Whether this is uncontrollable rage, or jealousy, or greed, or lust, our demons have the ability to make us do what is harmful to ourselves and possibly to others as well. For our purposes, it's important to note that violence—the stock in trade of all superheroes, vigilantes, and do-gooders—is a reflection of these demonic forces. May wrote that "violence is the daimonic gone awry . . . expressed in its most destructive form."[3]

We see one of the most interesting—and artistically rendered—examples of the demon/beast/shadow figure in comics in J. Michael Straczynski's *Midnight Nation*. *Midnight Nation* employs the conceit that there are two worlds, the world most of us live in and are aware of and a shadow world menaced by demonic figures; we discover that demons are humans who have been transformed ("turned") in the process of a long walk. David Grey, the hero of the work, is a cop who goes on the long walk with an angelic being called Laurel after he had been touched by a character we would probably call "Satan."

Along the way, David has to fight to keep his lower, more violent impulses inside, fight to keep from becoming one of the demons he and Laurel battle along their way to New York City. *Midnight Nation* is about many things, but it clearly touches on two spiritual issues central to this book: the problem of evil and the challenge of redemption. On the grand level of allegory, we can think of David's problem as the problem we all face after we've been touched by experience. We are aware of good and evil—and we can choose evil, even though it's bad for us, bad for society, bad for everything. Toward the end of the book, as David has been almost completely transformed into one of the demons, Laurel begs him to fight for his humanity—his goodness: "I know what you're feeling. Rage. Madness. Freedom. All at the same time. He exposed you to all those things to make you forget who you are. To make you forget you're a man."[4] In this brilliant and beautiful comic, David's fight for his humanity is set against a background of cosmic stories, good and evil, angels and devils. But ultimately, David prevails—keeps his soul, we might say—by being fully human.

The Hulk represents a long-running mainstream take on the problems we've been considering here. Jeff Jensen describes the character's genesis: "Back in Cold War '62, writer Stan Lee and artist Jack Kirby fused *Frankenstein* and *Dr. Jekylll and Mr. Hyde* with atomic heat and created an American *Godzilla*."[5] He's ugly, destructive—and all of that atomic bile boils up from within. Ang Lee, the director of *The Hulk*, was drawn to the character for just these reasons:

> "To me," says Lee, the filmmaker behind 1995's "Sense and Sensibility" and 2000's groundbreaking "Crouching Tiger, Hidden Dragon," "the Hulk is the manifestation of the part of yourself that you're trying to deny. . . . He's the big unknown that is hiding in the deepest level of brain structure—the reptile part of your brain."[6]

It's just this simple, as you probably know: When mild-mannered scientist Bruce Banner gets angry, frightened, or hurt, he turns into a gigantic green-skinned monster: the Hulk. And what does Hulk do? Well, in the immortal words of the monster himself, "Hulk smash." And, of course, the madder Hulk gets, the stronger Hulk gets. The Hulk becomes an almost unstoppable destructive demon (in the *Ultimates* version, the Hulk also has a little trouble ramping down his sexual desire), and Banner's great struggle over these many years has been to try to keep the Hulk down—and to deal with the guilt he feels for all the harm his demon has done when it has gotten free. (Hulk himself, particularly when he's portrayed as an intelligent being, feels less of this existential angst; he can't wish that he wasn't.)

The clawed X-Man Wolverine, likewise, carries inside himself a raging beast that wants to get out. The character's first appearances, interestingly enough, were in the pages of *The Hulk*, and from the beginning, they were marked by his so-called "berserker rages": in the heat of battle, Wolverine might—and sometimes did—lose control of himself, and with his razor-sharp claws, he was a lethal killing machine. Worse still, Wolverine was also uncertain about his past, which was largely blocked off from his memory—he knew he had done a lot of bad things, but he didn't by any means know all of them, although what he knew about was pretty horrible. Comic book historian Peter Sanderson sums

up the core of the character in this way: "Wolverine's greatest
enemy is himself. It has taken him years to master his animalistic
impulses to kill, and should his control slip, he could easily give
way to berserk madness."[7]

Wolverine's fits of animal rage leave even his friends, the
X-Men, unsettled and feeling alienated from him. After one of
Wolverine's casual displays of violence, the young Kitty Pryde
says to the other X-Men, "There are times, guys, when that
man scares me silly."[8] At one point in the seminal *Wolverine*
miniseries written by Chris Claremont and drawn by Frank
Miller, even Wolverine's great love, the Japanese Lady Mariko,
sees him in a feral rage and cannot stand what she sees. Her
father directs her to look closely at him: "The 'man' you profess
to love. Except that he is no man at all, but an animal cast in a
semblance of human form. . . . Gaze upon him, Mariko. Witness his true nature, his true self. Here is the . . . thing to which
you have given your heart." Mariko looks, and weighs what she
has seen—and rejects Wolverine.[9]

If those who love him most have trouble accepting his
darker impulses, then we can imagine that if Wolverine has any
sort of conscience—and he certainly does—then he too wrestles with these inner demons. Later in the Wolverine miniseries, Wolverine walks drunken and broken through the Ginza
District in Tokyo: "I didn't know it was possible to feel such
shame, to feel so sick at heart. I'm lost inside, my soul—all that
I thought I was, and am, and ever will be—shattered, cast to
the winds. Compared to this, death is a mercy."[10]

We can also think of Batman/Bruce Wayne as a character
battling the beast. As we saw in the chapter on vigilantes, there
are times that writers have taken Batman up to the edge of the
abyss, as in Jeph Loeb's Joker story in which Batman was prepared to kill the Joker, and brutally beat him bloody as a prel-
ude to that. Some writers treat Batman's violent methods and
dark demeanor only as trappings to spook the bad guys—a sort
of PG-rated Batman. But Paul Dini, another of Batman's writers, argues that the darkness is real, not just a costume: "Batman is cursed to seek salvation for a terrible sin he committed

in his past life, which in his mind was not being able to prevent the murder of his parents. Batman's war on crime is a symbolic war against himself."[11]

Connor Kent, the Superboy who first appeared in 1993 in the wake of Superman's death, eventually discovered that he had been cloned from both Superman and the archvillain Lex Luthor. It was a secret he tried to hide from even his closest friends, and after Luthor used him as a weapon to attack the Teen Titans, it eventually drove him to leave the Titans and hide out from the world on the Kents' farm. There he watched the beginning of the events that led to the Infinite Crisis, and while the world fell down around his ears, he was afraid to act—afraid that his dark side might reemerge.

In this battle against our darker side, we can all come to the point of desperation, of despair. We know what's right, and yet sometimes we fail, we fall, we turn the beast loose, and afterward we're filled with shame and remorse. The apostle Paul knew all about this. He wrote in the book of Romans that although he meant to do good, he often did evil instead, that there was something inside him that made him choose wrongly, that "something has gone wrong deep within me and gets the better of me every time."[12]

So what is the answer? How can we fight the beast? How do we express the beautiful divine nature we've been given instead of the dark and dangerous lower nature of the beast?

Well, in *Midnight Nation*, David Grey makes a supreme sacrifice, as heroes often do, to choose the higher good over his own personal good, out of a strong sense of hope in the face of despair. Other comics show us similar paths; even grumpy old Batman sometimes walks in light instead of shadow.

In *Soul War*, writer J. M. deMatteis let God's almost all-powerful servant, the Spectre (who is also Hal Jordan, the former Green Lantern), lay out the dimensions of Bruce Wayne's problem before showing us its solution:

He was born, I learned, out of a child's grief and sadness, and some said those emotions shattered his hold on sanity.

That the Batman was nothing but the costumed manifestation of a sick mind. The demon in his psyche—given free
rein. They didn't know him the way I finally did. He wasn't
madness and shadows. He was sanity and light clothed in
madness and shadows. . . . A good and decent man . . .
whose fierce morality and self-sacrificing nature . . . spoke
far more eloquently than the demon's mask . . . of who
Bruce Wayne really was. Sometimes, I think, even he wasn't
sure. Sometimes I think he believed the distorted images."[13]

During the events chronicled in *Soul War*, an apocalyptic
battle as much spiritual as it is physical, Bruce Wayne has to
wrestle with his demons: rage, pride, distrust, despair. At the
end, like David Gray, Batman chooses hope; he chooses faith;
he chooses belief. When the Spectre—who had been his friend
Hal Jordan before he became the villainous Parallax—seems to
have sacrificed himself for the sake of the earth, the distant and
cynical Batman has a moment of transformation, after which
he calls out to the Spectre:

> You were the best, the brightest, among us. When you fell—
> it . . . rattled me—and it made me wonder: If a man as good
> and decent as you could go wrong . . . what hope was there
> for the rest of us? But I see now—that one of the reasons
> you were reborn as the Spectre—was to give us all hope!"[14]

Likewise, in *Infinite Crisis*, Connor Kent fights the murder-
ous Superboy-Prime and foils the plans of Alexander Luthor to
alter reality—at the cost of his own life. When the chips are
down, his best nature emerges, and he stands alongside his
friends and mentors to do the right thing—no matter the cost.
In the moment of greatest darkness, he acts in hope—and saves
the world.

Salvation from despair comes from clinging to the higher
notions of hope and faith—in ourselves, in others, in a higher
power, in some kind of cosmic order. After Wolverine's moment
of despair in Tokyo, his dark night of the soul, he finds himself
in battle in a Zen garden. Afterward, bodies strewn everywhere,

the garden in disarray, order turned to chaos, he's drawn to kneel, to begin smoothing stones back into place, and it's then that he sees his hope:

> I may never be what I ought to be, want to be—but how will I know unless I try? Sure, it's scary, but what's the alternative? Stagnation—a safer, more terrible form of death. Not of the body. But of the spirit. An animal knows what it is, and accepts it. A man may know what he is, but he questions. He dreams. He strives. Changes. Grows. . . . I'm a man. . . . Not a beast. A man![15]

The battle against our beasts, our demons, our shadow selves can last our whole lives. But it's part of what makes us human. And we have spiritual resources that can aid us in the battle: the Eastern disciplines that Wolverine, Batman, and Daredevil studied, martial arts and meditation. Ritual and spiritual practice. And perhaps most important, there's faith in a higher power, one of the major tenets of the 12-step movement that began with Alcoholics Anonymous: If I'm going to get better, if I'm going to deal with this demon, I'm going to have to recognize that I don't have the power myself to fight it. Something much bigger than me will have to help. In my tradition, we call that power "God," and in one of the most stirring of the psalms, we hear this plea: "Out of the depths I cry to you, O Lord."[16]

Because we're human, we're always going to be imperfect; sometimes the beast is going to get out and wreak havoc. Wherever it is that evil originates in the universe, it is certain that evil makes its way into the world through our actions. We're involved daily in our own heroic fight against it. But our heroes—in comics, in literature, and ultimately in our spiritual traditions—can give us examples of how that battle can be won: through discipline, through faith, through self-sacrifice, and through hope.

The Apocalypse

Some say the world will end in fire
Some say in ice.
                    —"Fire and Ice," Robert Frost

Open just about any superhero comic over the past few years and what you'll see in many of them are world-threatening events and looming cosmic disaster: the Authority tries to keep a being so vast and powerful that it is referred to only as "God" from returning to take possession of its summer home—Earth; the Avengers must reverse Kang the Conqueror's conquest of the planet; Batman and Superman must avert world destruction as an asteroid chunk of Krypton falls into a collision course with Earth; the Ultimates battle an alien race who want to take over the world; the characters in *Powers* can only watch as a demented superman of almost limitless power destroys Utah, the Gaza Strip, and Vatican City; Superman fights a character named Doomsday; the X-Men wrestle with Apocalypse and his Four Horsemen; Thanos threatens to destroy All That Is with the Cosmic Cube or the Infinity Gauntlet or some other such cosmic doohickey; Hellboy is going to bring back the Elder Gods or usher in the end of the world; Galactus has come back to Earth, and he's hungry; and so on. And so on.

The end of the world is everywhere in superhero comics, because the end of the world *is* everywhere. Our fear of the end—and our hope—is part of the food we eat, the air we breathe. Lee Quinby writes,

> Americans have been taught to reside in apocalyptic terror and count on millennial perfection. For a substantial number, this is an intense Bible-based fundamentalism. For a larger majority, these fears and hopes are more nebulous, a loose blend of religious symbols and secular expression. In the United States, this imprecise yet overpowering belief system is a way of life.[1]

We sometimes believe—we fear—that the end of the world is upon us. But we are hardly the first to wrestle with these feelings. The branch of knowledge connected to the end of time is called "eschatology," from the ancient Greek words meaning "last discourse," and it's a pervasive part of not only our culture, but every culture we're familiar with. Comparative religionist Mircea Eliade wrote that "the myth of the end of the world is of universal occurrence," and Judeo/Christian thinking about the end of time has been going on for the past two thousand years, running from apocalyptic elements in the Hebrew Bible such as the book of Daniel to the prime material for many apocalyptic thinkers today, the book of Revelation in the New Testament.[2] And it all seems particularly relevant to us now, because of some changes that we've been through in recent years.

We have lived through some pretty scary times, with lots of signs that things are going bad: the Heaven's Gate, Branch Davidian, and other religious cults who let wild beliefs lead them to death or destruction; the domestic terrorism that destroyed the Murrah Federal building in Oklahoma City. We've seen the Y2K bug, which threatened to send us all back to the Stone Age—or at least back to the days before Microsoft; the fiery destruction of the World Trade Center in New York before our very eyes; kids killing kids at Columbine and in the classrooms of Virginia Tech, as well as in the streets of our inner cities; anthrax in our envelopes, AIDS across the planet, melting polar ice caps, El Niño, Hurricane Katrina, Darfur, and so it goes.

Things don't look good, and when things don't look good we can't help but ask ourselves, how is this all going to end? Our popular culture is one of the places where we try to answer those questions. We've noted briefly the omnipresent threat of world destruction in comics, and we'll return to this shortly. We can also point to the incredible popularity of the "Left Behind" books, written by evangelical Christians to explain their view of the end of the world. You don't have to be an evangelical Christian, believe in the particular interpretation of the book of Revelations advanced by authors Tim LaHaye and Jerry Jenkins, or even find the books well written to recognize their incredible popularity. It's rare indeed for a Christian title to travel outside the confines of Christian bookstores, let alone achieve *New York Times* best-seller status, yet all of the "Left Behind" books have done so. The books have sold well over 50 million copies worldwide and in the process inspired movies, dramatized versions, posters, and—for all I know—Underoos.

Clearly, these books tap into fears and hopes that are driving a lot of Americans. The widespread belief in a literal "rapture" and "tribulation" as described in the "Left Behind" series is a fairly recent theological development. You will search in vain for the word "rapture" in the Bible, and many religious historians point out that the rapture and its associated concepts have been a mainstream evangelical Christian concept for less than two hundred years. John Nelson Darby (1800–1882) tirelessly promoted these interpretations of the New Testament, and one of his disciples later integrated these teachings into the Scofield Reference Bible, which was incredibly popular among fundamentalist Christians in the last century. Yet polls taken in the past two decades indicate that despite our growing religious diversity, a majority of Americans still believe in a literal second coming of Jesus at the end of recorded time and in a decisive battle of Armageddon.[3] No wonder so many of us are frightened.

On a far less religious plane, we can also find insight about our fears in Michael Moore's Academy Award–winning documentary *Bowling for Columbine*, which uses a shotgun approach in trying to knock down America's current problems. But at the heart of almost everything Moore discusses—the arms race, the Columbine shootings, gun control—we find fear. Moore's interview with Professor Barry Glassner (whose book *The Culture of Fear* is a standard work on this subject) and interviews with average folks show that compared even to our close cousins across the Canadian border, Americans are a supremely fearful people. And it's this terror that apocalyptic culture taps into; we want to know what we're facing, and we want to believe that there's some hope. And it's here that our popular culture helps us.

It's also, as we'll see, where religion can help us. But first, let's look at a couple of the truly significant examinations of the apocalypse in comics to see how they've brought us comfort, and in what ways they agree with—and differ from—the religious solutions we'll find to these questions.

Few people who study popular culture would dispute the assertion that *Watchmen*, by Alan Moore and Dave Gibbons, is one of the landmark works of comic art. Today, twenty years after its publication, it's just as satisfying as—if less radical than—when it was first released. Moore's revisionist take on superheroes plants them squarely in a time and place where end-of-the-world scenarios were easy to entertain, the 1980s America of Ronald Reagan, who famously made jokes about declaring nuclear war on Russia. Instead of Reagan, Moore has returned Richard Nixon to the Oval Office, with Henry Kissinger at his side—a fearsome pair of warmongers—and played off the long history of comics by acknowledging that once there were groups of crime fighters who have since been disbanded by antivigilante laws, all except for the government operatives: the Comedian, killed in the first pages of the book; the superpowered Dr. Manhattan; and the unrepentant vigilante Rorshach.

The mood throughout *Watchmen* is one of tangible despair and fear; except for Dr. Manhattan—so powerful that he can alter human history, but also so powerful that he has little interest in it—there seems to be nothing standing between the world and imminent nuclear destruction as the United States and Russia stand toe to toe, posturing over the country of Afghanistan (once invaded by the Russians, recently invaded by the United

States). Rorshach records in his journal at the outset, "Now the whole world stands on the brink, staring down into bloody Hell," and although Rorshach isn't exactly an advertisement for sanity, he speaks for almost every character we encounter in the book, major and minor. He may be the paranoid herald of judgment day, but judgment day is coming all the same. When he tells us "soon there will be war. Millions will burn. Millions will perish in sickness and misery," we believe him.[4]

The choice of images speaks as loudly as the dialogue about the impending doom: a yellow happy-face button with a disturbing crimson splatter of blood on it; the three-triangled radiation danger symbol; a clock with its hands approaching midnight; entwined lovers who appear as shadows on a wall— or as skeletons; an atomic mushroom cloud; and then, in the last chapter of the book, the first full-panel drawings. In those six full-page drawings, we are invited—forced, really—to witness the horrifying destruction of half of New York City, the apocalypse we've been rushing toward with anticipation and dread throughout the book.

One of the strengths of the book is how it critiques much of our conventional thinking. The architect of New York City's destruction is not some supervillain, Russia, or some cosmic threat. Instead it is a superman, Ozymandias, formerly a crime fighter and now the world's smartest, most physically advanced human being. He murders the Comedian, has Dr. Manhattan exiled, and kills millions in New York City with an elaborate hoax of an alien invasion—all part of his plan to save the world from that impending nuclear destruction.

And it works; terrified by Ozymandias's fake alien incursion, Russia pulls out of Afghanistan and agrees to work with America in making peace so that human beings can repulse any further attacks from beyond. Ozymandias has saved the world, and everyone who knows the truth—even though they have tremendous reservations—agrees to be quiet. As in much of apocalyptic literature, where there is a sense that something good will follow the judgment day, he tells them, "I saved Earth from Hell. Next, I'll help her toward Utopia."[5]

Some of the characters in *Watchmen* find comfort—and meaning—in human love and connection. Dr. Manhattan strikes off for the stars, content to leave things as they are. But Rorshach won't—can't—buy into these solutions. One of the central ironies of the book is that this pathetic little man also has an unbending sense of right and wrong, and while it is often misguided, there is something admirable about his credo: "There is good and there is evil, and evil must be punished. Even in the face of Armageddon I shall not compromise in this."[6] And he doesn't; at the book's end, we are left with the sense that thanks to Rorshach, perhaps all of Ozymandias's machinations will be exposed after all.

We are also left with Moore's sense that perhaps we have set ourselves an artificial dilemma with all this talk of Armageddon. Dr. Manhattan is the godlike figure of the book, immensely powerful, capable of experiencing past and future at the same time; without being conceited, he tells Ozymandias at one point that the latter's being the world's smartest human "means no more to me than does its smartest termite."[7] In his last appearance in *Watchmen*—before he goes off, perhaps to create some human life of his own—he tells Ozymandias, "Nothing ends, Adrian. Nothing ever ends."[8]

In a sense, for all our fear of "the end," he's right. Ancient cultures thought of history as circular, an endless repetition of seasons and events; physicists sometimes talk about the history of our universe as cyclical, beginning with the Big Bang that brought it into being, then its expansion until forces can no longer support it and its collapse, and someday in the far distant future, another Big Bang. But as we'll see shortly when we talk about what faith has to say about the mysterious beginning of things—and the equally mysterious end—these are things that we want to have been planned by somebody, not just to happen arbitrarily.

Another recent examination of the apocalypse—and one that even more powerfully evokes familiar religious metaphors—is DC's *Kingdom Come,* by Mark Waid and Alec Ross. Ross, whose father is a minister, actually painted his father into the book as the lead character, minister Norman McKay. The story also features God's messenger, the Spectre, as a major character, and the story begins with—and often returns to—lines from the book of Revelation about the end of days.

What makes *Kingdom Come* such a compelling work is not just Ross's amazing paintings or the spectacle of generations of superhumans in battle; at its heart, *Kingdom Come* is a book about faith and belief, that there truly are reasons that things happen—even horrific things—and that all is ordained to turn out well. Although it rarely preaches, *Kingdom Come* is one of the most religious comics ever published.

As with *Watchmen*, *Kingdom Come* shows us a world on the brink of disaster, although here it isn't human but superhuman activity that threatens all there is. It is a world without a Superman. Faced with the growing savagery of the new generation of "heroes," Superman has retired to solitude, taking his power and his influence out of a world that desperately needs it, and that is, as always, an unsettling thought. Alex Ross is one of the vast number of writers and artists who have seen Superman as a Christ figure: "To me, Superman as a fictional character is just as important as if he existed in flesh and blood—either way he is inspirational, and that's what's relevant."[9] And when Superman's inspiration is pulled out of that world, the results are disastrous: the other members of the Justice League also step back from human affairs, and the metahumans left behind struggle for supremacy, often with cataclysmic results. As the Spectre tells Norman McKay, "The gods of yesterday no longer walk among the humans. . . . Instead, cued by Superman's surrender, they journey apart."[10] And without their stabilizing influence, the world is at the mercy of forces beyond its control.

It is a world strangely without hope, perched on the edge of disaster, and Pastor McKay's guided tour of the state of things at the side of the Spectre leaves him deeply disturbed. "You're an angel! That makes you a messenger of hope! . . . A greater power sent you! Your very existence is a testimony to faith! You mean that all you have to tell me is that those who could save us won't?"[11]

Is the world truly abandoned by God—and by the gods of justice? Are McKay's visions of apocalypse to come true? As the notes to the story indicate, "Since our world is one of shattered faith where gods walk the streets and throw buses at one another, McKay has been shaken from most everything in which he once believed."[12] It is in the land of despair where we begin most such tales. But in the course of the story, the main characters—Norman McKay, Superman, and others—regain their faith and sense of purpose.

It's not that people don't get killed, that destruction on a massive scale doesn't take place, that in a sense, the world doesn't end. All of those things take place. It's just that all of those events happen for a reason—which is what apocalyptic literature always tells us. At the end of the story, good and order have been restored, the world has moved into a new phase, and the characters—and maybe we readers—have learned some lessons.

Norman McKay asks the Spectre at one horrible point in the book why he can't just intervene, stop things, change things, and the Spectre reminds him, "There will be a reckoning, Norman McKay. Be prepared. As the scriptures say, 'Fear God, and give glory to him, for the hour of his judgment has come.'"[13]

Here is what has always been at the heart of apocalyptic literature: the sense that there is a plan, that all is going as it is supposed to, that somebody knows what's going on even if it looks to us like the world is going to hell in a handbasket. Val J. Sauer Jr. eloquently sums up the appeal of thinking eschatologically from a faith perspective:

> Faced with the possibility of an atomic war, the reality of death, and the threat of ecological disaster, biblical eschatology assures the Christian that a loving God has not abandoned his creation. Creation and redemption, the beginning and end of history, are acts of God. Biblical eschatology declares that history is moving toward an ultimate goal, the redemption of creation.[14]

It's this sort of redemptive eschatology we find working in *Kingdom Come*: things work out after all. Superman learns that he can't turn his back on the human side of himself; Norman McKay recovers his faith and discovers there is something he can do: he can give people hope.

Hope is the flip side of doomsday; we want to believe that not only is there a plan for things, but it's a plan that leads us to a better existence. As Jan Quinby points out, "What makes living with apocalyptic belief tolerable for so many is its accompanying millennial dream, the current of hope that promises the fullness of Truth unveiled."[15] Unlike what Quinby calls "endism" (the fear-based response to impending threats that we find in most comics, where the simple goal is to prevent the end of everything), most of us yearn for some sort of "electism," the idea that those who are worthy (good, faithful) will be chosen to survive into some new peaceful, joyful existence—whether that existence is on a new earth, in heaven, or something for which we don't yet even have a name.

Kingdom Come ends as it began, with Norman McKay. He stands in front of his congregation, and he preaches again from the book of Revelation. But much has changed as a result of the events of the story, and McKay preaches a new message, a message of hope gained from his experiences with the Spectre, God's messenger: "That a dream is not always a prophecy. That the future, like so much else, is open to interpretation. And that hope is brightest when it dawns from fear."[16]

At the end of *Kingdom Come*, Norman has regained his faith, and for people of faith, our response to the world must always be one of hope. If we believe that God has a plan to redeem creation, then the world is always moving past its current difficulties to a more perfect future. The rhetoric of the civil rights movement often used this model for its effect; remember Dr. Martin Luther King Jr.'s "I Have a Dream" speech?

But hope must always be more that just a vague desire for things to turn out right. As Dr. King's example reminds us, hope is an active quality. "Because hope is much more than a mood," says theologian John Polkinghorne, "it involves a commitment to action. Its moral character implies that what we hope for should be what we are prepared to work for and so bring about."[17] The book of Revelation can give both a sense of impending doom, as it does at the beginning of *Kingdom Come*, and a message of comfort, as it does at the end.

This is what ultimately makes both *Kingdom Come* and *Watchmen* such powerful tales of apocalypse; even against the cosmic scale of events, both make us believe that human action matters. Rorshach's journal may turn the course of history after he is dead and gone, and Norman McKay's preaching shares the new sense of joy, mission, and hope he's gained.

Like them, although we can influence events, we can't control them; we may not, in fact, even understand them. But we can believe. And we can act.

How the world ends is not up to us. But what we do while we're in it? That part most certainly is.

The Holocaust

I have wept over too many graves.
                    —Magneto, in "God Loves, Man Kills"

The movie begins with cattle cars. Railroad cars full of people, bedraggled, hungry, frightened. They have arrived at a camp where they're treated like cattle, separated like cattle, and soon, they will be executed like cattle.

Their captors wear gray uniforms and speak brutally. They separate families, mothers and sons. But one son will not go quietly. And when he resists—resists with all his might—he is dealt with violently.

These scenes are achingly familiar, but they are not drawn from *Schindler's List* or any of the other Holocaust films and documentaries you have seen. It is the beginning of the first *X-Men* film (1999), and the graphic comparison between these haunted outcasts and others to come is made particularly real because the little boy we see here will grow up to become the archvillain Magneto. And then, after he has become an adult, he will see his people hunted, not because of anything they have done, but simply because of the blood that runs in their veins.

Not all stories of the end of things are fiction. In the twentieth century, the human race did manage to dodge total oblivion from many of the big world-enders: atomic weapons, poison gas, biological agents, natural disasters, famine. But there was one twentieth-century disaster that hit full on, one world that was almost completely ended, one set of villains whose evil plans weren't thwarted by the forces of justice and democracy.

Between 1933, when Adolph Hitler came to power, and 1945, when Nazi Germany was defeated, the Holocaust destroyed almost all the Jews of Eastern Europe, many from Western Europe, as well as Gypsies, homosexuals, intellectuals, and political dissidents—well over six million people dead. It's one of the greatest human tragedies of history, made all the more disturbing because it was a systematic attempt at genocide carried out by a civilized Christian nation, and we are still trying to deal with the implications of the Holocaust today in such widely scattered venues as politics, theology, and popular culture.

For the Jews, the question of how God could let such a thing happen has shaped their contemporary theology, while the fear of such a thing happening again has shaped the politics of the nation of Israel toward the Palestinians with whom they share the land, and toward their Arab neighbors. For Christians, their complicity in the anti-Semitism that undergirded the Holocaust has led to hard questions about responsibility, religious intolerance, and interfaith relations. For people of all persuasions, the question has only been complicated by other attempts at genocide in this century, in places as far-flung as Cambodia, Rwanda, Bosnia, and Darfur.

Is it part of our nature to try and destroy people who are different from us? How can we be aware of these feelings—and stop genocide from happening again on such a grand scale? As with other momentous questions, comics have turned the problem over and come up with some answers, if we're only willing to look.

Perhaps the most obvious example of comics responding to the Holocaust comes with a two-volume work by Art Spiegelman, *Maus* and *Maus II*. No other comic or graphic novel has ever received such mainstream critical acclaim: *Maus* is the only comic ever to win the coveted Pulitzer Prize, and both volumes were also nominated for the National Book Critics Circle

Award—for biography. Because, you see, *Maus* is based on a series of interviews that Spiegelman did with his father Vladek, a Holocaust survivor, and the story he tells is our entry into a world so horrific that a story is really the only way to begin to comprehend it.

Spiegelman also made a controversial artistic choice: rather than draw the comic in a realistic way, he decided to make the different groups different funny animals. So the Jews are mice, the Nazis cats, and the Poles are pigs. Some people thought this underground comic convention trivialized the story, but most critics disagreed. As Don Markstein puts it, "Maybe the subject needs trivialization, just so the reader can wrap his mind around it. Nothing in the average person's experience can prepare him for images of human beings behaving that way."[1] In practice, the "funny animal" trope just gives us a bit of distance; it doesn't dehumanize Vladek or make his story less interesting or important. In fact, in some ways, the image of the Jews as mice at the mercy of the cats enhances our emotional response. We get a heightened sense of their danger, at all times, even when the cats seem to be playing nice.

What pulls us into the history of the Holocaust is the same thing that draws us in the example from X-Men at the beginning of the chapter; history becomes more accessible when we get to know the people involved in it. Otherwise, it's just bleak statistics. In *Maus*, Spiegelman tells us of the brutality, the narrow escapes, but he also tells us the human stories of his parents' courtship, and when his father protests that "This has nothing to do with Hitler, with the Holocaust!" Art tells his father, "Pop—It's great material. It makes everything more real—more human."[2]

It's the human story that *Maus* is most concerned with; the philosophical and spiritual questions are left to other comics to deal with. It's enough—sometimes too much—just to walk in the shoes of this Holocaust survivor, to see the German death squads bashing the heads of Jewish children against the stone, to come to the gates of Auschwitz concentration camp and its famous gate with the slogan "Arbeit Macht Frei" (Work Will

Make You Free) and hear Vladek say, "And we knew that from here we will not come out anymore. We knew the stories—that they will gas us and throw us in the ovens. This was 1944 . . . we knew everything. And here we were."[3]

Other comics have dealt with the larger implications of the Holocaust, using it as the basis for stories or story elements. Concentration camps and death camps have often been depicted in comic books—including the internment camp for "bad" metahumans in *Kingdom Come* and a camp established by aliens for all superheroes in the relaunch of *Justice League of America*. But as I suggested in the beginning of this chapter, one comic title has consistently wrestled with the human and spiritual issues of the Holocaust in story after story: the X-Men.

In the 1960s, when the original series debuted, it may have been that the mutant identity of the X-Men was more closely attuned to race than anything else. The X-Men were "feared by a world they were sworn to save," which sounds pretty similar to the ongoing fear and contempt some Gentiles have had for the Jews, who believe they have a special covenant with God passed down through his agreement with Abraham that through him and his descendants "all the families of the Earth will be blessed."[4]

As time has passed, though, in the decades since the first issue of *The Uncanny X-Men*, the themes of prejudice and oppression dealt with in the X-Men stories have expanded to include all people who are treated differently because of who they are. (Witness the film *X-2*, in which, after Bobby Drake "comes out" to his parents about being a mutant, his mother asks, "Have you tried not being a mutant?") As Chris Claremont wrote in his afterword to "God Loves, Man Kills," "Mutants in the Marvel Universe have always stood as a metaphor for the underclass, the outsiders; they represent the ultimate minority."[5] Being hated and persecuted simply because of who or what you are has become the grounding tension in the X-Men stories, and over and over again, the story lines draw the link between the prejudice the X-Men face and Hitler's Final Solution.

The X-Men spin-off *Weapon X* makes the comparison obvious: one story line centers on young mutant Billy Taylor, who is taken with his family to the mutant detention center called Neverland. The imagery is drawn directly from Holocaust films and photos: brutal guards, guard towers, lines of people standing in the snow waiting to be processed, tattoos. Billy overhears one of the characters in the camp making the comparison explicit: "This was modern day America, she shouted, not Nazi Germany!"[6]

But the camp is what it seems, and in a one-page spread of panels done almost without words, the point of view alternates between Billy looking through a window where the guards have taken a group of mutants who've been separated and led away—and his reaction: shock, horror, tears. Billy sees what is going to happen to every mutant in Neverland who gets taken away from the others, and we can imagine that this is what a young Jewish boy would have seen—and felt—in Auschwitz. As with *Maus*, the story takes us into the horror of a single involved person—but it also grapples with the idea that genocide isn't just a German idea; it can happen anywhere that people are so frightened by other people that they don't recognize their common humanity. In the biting summary of this way of thinking by priest and activist Thomas Merton: "It is enough to affirm one basic principle: ANYONE BELONGING TO CLASS X OR NATION Y OR RACE Z IS TO BE REGARDED AS SUBHUMAN AND WORTHLESS, AND CONSEQUENTLY HAS NO RIGHT TO EXIST. All the rest will follow without difficulty."[7]

The persecution and hunting down of mutants has been a longtime motif in the X-Men stories, with an entire line of superrobots, the Sentinels, created solely for that purpose. The Sentinels have cropped up now and again over the years as tools employed by mutant-hating human beings, but never more powerfully than in "Days of Future Past," originally published in *Uncanny X-Men* 141–42 in 1980. In these two issues, a guest visits the X-Men from an apocalyptic future where almost all of the X-Men have been killed, and gives a view of the holocaust that awaits all mutantkind if things go on unchanged. (And that view is shown again in the days following the "House of M" story line, as Sentinels ring Professor Xavier's school, making it a virtual concentration camp.)

That visitor is the only Jewish X-Man (-Woman), Kitty Pryde, and she comes from a future of genocide where classes of people are defined by the letter they wear on their clothes (like Jews in the streets of Germany emblazoned with the yellow Star of David to set them apart), and mutants survive only inside internment camps. As she walks back into the camp where she lives, she passes the gravestones of most of the X-Men—and many of the other, nonmutant heroes of the Marvel Universe, whom the Sentinels have killed for good measure.

It is a haunting scene.

Equally haunting is the public hearing Senator Robert Kelly has convened at the Capitol to discuss "the mutant question." He is, we're told, a decent man, but he fears that mutants are so different from *Homo sapiens* that their coexistence is impossible. During his opening speech, Dr. Moira McTaggert leans over to tell Charles Xavier (Professor X), "If you ask me, Charles, that sod's already made up his mind. Registration of mutants today, gas chambers tomorrow."[8] As we've seen, it's too short a step from fear to persecution to attempted extermination.

The graphic novel *Man Loves, God Kills*, a major source for *X-2*, also spotlights mutants persecuted for no other reason than the blood that flows in their veins. In the first pages of the book, a boy and girl flee their armed pursuers—the Purifiers, they call themselves—and when they're trapped in a school playground and the boy is shot, the little girl can only look up wide-eyed and ask, "Why?"

"Because you have no right to live," is the answer, and when both children are dead, the Purifiers hang them up, with a sign reading "Muties" like a Star of David to indicate their offense.

They are meant to be an example, but they are discovered and taken down by one who has seen this before—Magneto, the little boy who survived the death of his family in the Nazi death camps, only to become part of a modern world pursuing a new persecution. He is heartbroken, tenderly touching their corpses, and saying, "So young . . . so innocent . . . to know such terror and pain. Their only crime—that they had been born."[9]

One of the reasons Magneto is such a driven character—and a villain in the eyes of most of the world—is that he has power, and he will not willingly see such a thing happen again. The admonition to Jews to remember—"Never again!"—is one which Magneto takes seriously. In the words of Sir Ian McKellen, who plays him in the films, "Even if he's evil . . . you can see that he's doing things for a reason. He's trying to protect his people."[10] When the comic-book Magneto takes over the nation of Genosha and establishes it as a homeland for mutants, it seems a clear analogy for the Jewish experience after World War II, the establishment of Israel in Palestine in 1948. Here, at least, they might think, we can be safe from people who would kill us for no other reason than who we are.

Magneto's solution has always been separation and open antagonism—and the use of force, if necessary. But although the X-Men have had to fight over and over again, they have never embraced Magneto's solutions, and unlike many comics, "God Loves, Man Kills" ends not with force resolving the issue, but with words. Cyclops tells his fellow mutants that it isn't the Purifiers who are dangerous, but the ideas they represent. "If we don't stand up to those . . . then all we've done is delay an inevitable holocaust."[11]

So Cyclops and the Rev. Stryker, the force behind the Purifiers, face off in front of a crowd in Madison Square Garden, and Cyclops answers Stryker's charges that "whatever a man's color or beliefs, he is still human. Those children—and you X-Men—are not!"[12] Labels, names, categories; they are things we use to try and understand where things fit. But they can be dangerous, especially when we assign them to people and then think less of them because of the labels we've given them.

Many of the Jews who suffered through the death camps—or have reflected on them since—have suffered a profound crisis of faith. *After Auschwitz*, the influential book by Jewish theologian Richard Rubenstein, argues that if there was a covenant between Jews and God before the Holocaust, it clearly no longer exists. God, if God exists, didn't lift a finger to stop things; henceforth, the only thing Jews can rely on is themselves, and so they had better pursue power at all costs. Charles Xavier suffers a similar crisis of faith because of the public persecution presented in "God Loves, Man Kills." He almost steps away from his lifelong belief that humans and mutants can live together in peace and embraces Magneto's solution, violence and terror. Again Cyclops has to intervene, this time to remind Xavier how they differ from that vision of imposing order through force. To use the methods of evil men is to become like them—and to treat people as different, as evil, because of what they believe instead of trying to engage them through their shared humanity is to fail every ideal he taught them.

Chris Claremont wrote that, for him, the "crux of the conflict" in the graphic novel came from these questions: "Are we all in some manner or shape or form children of God? Or are some of us perhaps more beloved than others? . . . We need to cherish that which binds us, and accept with a measure of tolerance some of the things that make us different," but he concluded sadly, that although twenty years had passed since the comic first appeared, "people are still judged more by the color of their skin, and the nation of their origin, and the faith they espouse, than their character."[13]

It's tragic. And true. Although Buddhists speak of cultivating compassion for all living things, although the book of Galatians in the New Testament reminds us that because of Jesus there are no distinctions between us, although Archbishop Desmond Tutu speaks of "the Rainbow People of God," the truth is that too many of us haven't yet attained this understanding that we are all linked. The X-Men stories remind us of the ultimate horror of prejudice and intolerance: that over and over again, we persecute and kill people just because they differ from us. And those who survive such persecution? Well, the survivors of the Holocaust—and the leaders of Israel today—seem too often to wind up like Magneto: They refuse to weep over any more graves. Only power will suffice. So they kill those who would kill them, and so on. And so forth.

It's an ever-spiraling cycle of hatred and violence, and sometimes it seems that there's no way out.

But, thank God, there is.

The End of Violence

Compassion is apocalypse, the true revolution, the end of
warfare and the politics of power.
                    —Sam Keen, *To Love and Be Loved*

It's just after 9/11, and the towers have fallen. So have a lot of
other things: America's sense of security, our confidence that
terror is something that only happens in the Gaza Strip or
Northern Ireland. Not Manhattan. Please, God, not Manhattan. But amid the wreckage of the World Trade Center, a lone
man sorts through the rubble, all the while thinking as furi-
ously as he moves, "We've got to be strong—Stronger than
we've ever been. If we lose hope here—Bury our faith in this
darkness—Then nothing else matters."

The man is Steve Rogers—Captain America—and when his
sometime boss Nick Fury orders him onto a plane bound for
Kandahar to initiate a violent response to this violent act,
Rogers refuses.

"Look around," he tells Fury. "They need me. The ones who
might have five minutes of breath or blood left before they die."[1]

As we've seen in other chapters, the typical superhero
response—OK, the typical human response—to pain, to violence, to terror, is to react. To strike back. To end the threat violently, as violently as need be. But Cap is rethinking that formula,
even in these times of challenge.

On his way home from working in the wreckage, Steve Rogers meets an Arab American youth, Samir, on the streets of the city, and he encourages him to get in off the streets. It's late, and he may not be safe out there alone. Steve Rogers knows that human nature is to see Samir not as an individual, but as a nationality, a skin color, at least in the wake of what has happened to the Twin Towers and the Pentagon. Captain America, as you may know, saw the Nazi death camps during World War II; he knows a little bit about the dark side of our nature.

And sure enough, a drunk man who has lost someone in the disaster sees Samir, and he doesn't see Samir as another grieving New Yorker.

He sees an enemy who is somehow responsible for the death of Jenny, someone he loved, and he pulls a knife and moves forward.

And he would have his revenge—what he may imagine is justice—except that Steve Rogers has stepped in between the knife and its intended victim. And he's done so not as Steve Rogers, but clad now in the costume of Captain America.

As the knife splinters on his red, white, and blue shield, Cap is brought back again to the challenge that faces us:

> We've got to be stronger than we've ever been. Or they've won. We can hunt them down. We can scour every blood-stained trace of their terror from the Earth. We can turn every stone they've ever touched to dust, and every blade of grass to ash. And it won't matter. We've got to be stronger than we've ever been—as a people. As a nation. We have to be America. Or they've won.[2]

And what does it mean to be America in the wake of all this? The following pages of the story suggest a possibility. When Cap asks the assailant about Jenny, and tells the man that he knows he wants justice, he also tells him, "This isn't justice. We're better than this."

And in turn, Samir approaches the man, speaks to him, tells him how sorry he is about Jenny.

As Cap walks away, they are shaking hands, joined in their common humanity, their common loss.[3]

This response—that of compassion, of love, of faith, of trust—is the one we'll examine in this chapter. Since 9/11, the comics industry has begun to wrestle with the legacy of violence and revenge that has always fueled superhero comics, reflecting that human response: You hurt me; I'm going to hurt you.

But we can do better. And we must.

One of the comics collected in the first volume of *9–11: Artists Respond* is a short story written by Mark Carey called "The House of Light." In the story, Pete, a building contractor, is planning to leave his wife Frieda, who has apparently betrayed him with another man, and not even the traumatic events of 9/11 will change his mind. As they talk in the middle of the night, he says that there is nothing to be done, and she answers in a way that takes him aback: "We can love each other."

No way, he says. The world doesn't work that way.

"That's not what I mean," Frieda says, and she is weeping. "It's what people do when it all falls apart, Pete. If they care about what they've lost. They put it back together."

But he still shakes his head. "No. What people do is they hit back. When someone's hurt you, you've got the right to do that."[4] And it's clear that they've gone from talking just about the attacks on New York and Washington to their own private pain. But the two options are just as real on the personal level as they are on the political: love or hate. That's what it all boils down to.

We saw in the previous chapter how Jews with the legacy of the Holocaust in their rearview mirror created a powerful nation that could defend itself against all comers—and which, in the process, herded Palestinians into prisons and detention centers, responded to violence with even greater violence, and vowed to defend itself no matter what the cost.

My colleague and friend at Baylor University, Jewish theologian Marc Ellis, has devoted his life to the unpopular position of arguing that the nation of Israel has a responsibility not to let its actions be determined by the violence done to Jews before its creation. He has written about visiting Palestinian children in a Jerusalem hospital who were injured by Israeli soldiers, and how he realized then that Israel's use of violent force was a moral wrong eerily similar to those wrongs that Jews had endured in the Holocaust and other anti-Semitic attacks throughout history; he realized that Israel had become an oppressor instead of the force for justice called for in the Hebrew Bible. "By seeing power as the only way forward," he writes, "by feeling that with power comes dignity and respect, by projecting power as the only line of defense against a further violation, another holocaust," Jews were losing their sense of justice, of rightness, of covenant.[5] Yes, they were saving their nation. But they were losing their selves, their souls, in the process.

OK, you say. What else can they do? The Palestinians attack Jews daily. What's the solution? Well, another post-9/11 comic addresses that very question.

The first panel introduces the setting: "Yad Vashem Holocaust Museum, Jerusalem. Today." Into this setting walks a Palestinian suicide bomber. And you can guess the rest—explosion, carnage, death. One of the dead is a little girl, daughter of an Israeli fighter pilot named Sholem, and when he gets the news, he clearly thinks he knows exactly what he should do: "A Palestinian madman has taken my daughter from me forever. Nothing can make me feel better about this. Nothing less than an eye for an eye." When his wife protests that she doesn't want the blood of someone else's children on his hands, it stops him in his tracks. But does it change his mind?

The pilot, Sholem, boards his plane for a clearly unauthorized mission, swoops low over the bomber's village, then over the city of Tel Aviv. When the jet fighter dives on Tel Aviv, there is a powerful, heart-breakingly human scene as an Arab mother looks up, sees impending death in the diving plane, and gathers her children to her. "Don't look," she tells them. "Close your eyes. Come here to me. Come here to me, my darlings. I love you. I love you so much."

But they don't die. Instead, there is the flap and flutter of paper. And suddenly we see the amazing truth. This Israeli pilot hasn't dropped bombs; he has dropped leaflets. And the mothers in both village and city pick them up to read, "You killed my daughter." A picture of Sholem's little girl, laughing, accompanies this caption. And on the back of the paper: "I could have killed yours. We must stop now, before you know my pain."[6]

This project, *411*, was conceived by Marvel Comics in the wake of 9/11. As Bill Jemas, then the president and chief operating officer of Marvel, wrote in his introduction, all the stories submitted for the anthology, no matter what their genesis, had a common theme: "Your enemy, even your mortal enemy, is a member of the family of man . . . a member of *your* own family. . . . *411* is about peacemakers; people who make sacrifices in the name of humanity."[7]

It was a particularly daring message to spread after 9/11, because as Jemas pointed out, in wartime any suggestion that the enemy is human, like us instead of wholly other, can be regarded as disloyal. It's important to hate what we fear, especially in wartime. As Catholic priest and theologian Richard Rohr has said, "Hate makes the world go around. Once you have a specific thing to hate, it takes away your fear."[8] And throughout our history, Americans have felt better when they had an enemy to hate: England, Germany, the Soviet Union. Now, Islamic terrorists—or anyone who looks like he or she might be one.

But as Captain America said, we have to be better than that. To do better. Because clearly, hatred is not only morally wrong but it's damaging to us personally. Cormac McCarthy, in his novel *Cities of the Plain*, wrote with wisdom about what hatred does to us individually, even if we are the so-called victims of those we hate:

Our enemies . . . seem always with us. The greater our hatred the more persistent the memory of them so that a truly terrible enemy becomes deathless. So that the man who has done you great injury or injustice makes himself a guest in your house forever. Perhaps only forgiveness can dislodge him.[9]

So the choice is clear: hatred or love. Ever-escalating violence or—

What?

In *Amazing Spider-Man* #36, the official Marvel response to 9/11, J. Michael Straczynski's script sounds notes of grief, bravery, and bluster; it also speaks of a voice we must listen to even as we respond to the attacks: "The voice that says all wars have innocents. The voice that says you are a kind and a merciful people. The voice that says do not do as they do, or the war is lost before it is even begun."[10]

In another of the stories in the first *9-11 Artists Respond* collection, Alan Moore also affirms the voice of compassion. In the opening panels of the story "This Is Information," we pull closer to a scene of devastation and a hand jutting from the rubble. Hold that information; it'll be important. The story is about what we learn, how we learn, and even whether we learn. Coming forward from the Crusades to the Islamic terrorists' idea of jihad, Moore wrestles with the ongoing idea of evil, of just and holy wars, of the idea that things can only be black and white, good or evil. "Dazed and confused as we are in the rubble of our towers," Moore tells us, "there is an opportunity to learn something here. Perhaps just one opportunity. And yet we are all, supposedly, [either] with the crusaders or the terrorists."

Then we return to that hand, forlorn, lonely, jutting up from the rubble, and Moore reaches the same decision as Steve Rogers: "With all due respect, with all sympathy, with all love, some of us cannot make that choice. Are we with the terrorists or the crusaders? No," he says, as a living hand extends into the panel to touch the hand sticking up from the rubble. "No. We're with you. Whoever you are."[11]

Moore tells us in this story that the choice between good and evil, between us and them may be satisfying, but it's a false choice. Our hands need to be extended to those who are suffering, whoever they may be. But that can be a hard lesson for us to hold.

We love violence just as much as we love hatred. Nations around the world are amazed that we Americans raise a fuss about movies with naked people in them but let our children watch explicit violence that they consider pornographic. I remember an occasion some years back when a good friend and I let our two little boys watch one of the *Lethal Weapon* films. I remember putting my hand over my son Jake's eyes when a woman took her top off, but not once did I cover his eyes as the good guys perforated the bad guys in interesting ways. We love violence, and especially when it comes in the guise of justice. So in a movie like *Spider-Man* or *Daredevil*—as in most of our films—we don't want to see the bad guy just led off in hand-cuffs. We want to see him perforated.

And yet not all of our popular culture calls for us to vio-lently eliminate what we fear. Superman, again, can teach us something. By now, this shouldn't be a surprise to us. But remember the ongoing debate we considered about the level of violence necessary to subdue evildoers? I can't escape the image of Superman, who over the years not only benefited from his invulnerable hide, but also from the array of talents he could employ against violent offenders. Gangsters emptied their guns against his chest, or he melted their guns with a glance from his heat vision, or he blew them into a jail cell with his super breath, or with a precisely modulated blow, he dealt out just the smallest amount of force necessary to control the situation. A Wolverine, a Punisher—sometimes even a Batman—would have used force, maybe lots of it. But clearly, Superman again stands in for us as a messianic figure of justice and peace.

Is this ridiculous? Not at all. British comics writer Alan Moore has talked about how, in a family (in fact, a nation) largely unformed by organized religion, the heroes in comics helped to define morality for him. My mechanic, Andy (yes, I was on a first-name basis with the guy who fixed my string of used Volvos), and I agreed that although we both grew up in religious families (his dad was a minister, in fact), Superman and Spider-Man and Captain America taught us many things about how we were supposed to live. And in the second volume of *9-11*, Brian K. Vaughan wrote a story that reinforces the idea that comics can have an impact on who we are.

The story begins with a comic artist inking that iconic pose of Superman with an American flag, one of the best-known associations in the comics world, then putting down his brush.

"I can't do this," Vince, the artist, tells his father. After watching the towers fall from his rooftop, he can't see the point anymore in drawing comics—in anything, in fact, so frivolous as entertainment or art. "What's the point of drawing guys in capes and tights now?"

His dad rubs his chin and looks up from his own work—penciling a comic strip. "Whatever you want it to be," he says. And he reminds Vince, "Aren't you the one who says reading all those Superman comics when you were a kid made you what you are today? . . . You're always telling folks that the world has to find a way to solve its problems without killing. Don't you think those characters helped shape that outlook?"[12]

So let's learn what we're supposed to learn. If we can learn our morality from the Punisher or Superman, I choose Superman. (I'm not talking, again, about the dramatic excitement of the bad guy getting what's coming to him, in whatever violent form that might be; I'm saying that if we're going to look at comics for wisdom, here's where we're going to find it.)

In *A Superman for All Seasons*, writer Jeph Loeb and artist Tim Sales give us a series of panels in which Superman floats outside the penthouse office of his archenemy Lex Luthor. Superman could reduce Luthor to ashes with his heat vision; he could shatter every bone in his body; he could jerk that bald head off Luthor's body and hurl it into orbit.[13]

But you may notice how my even mentioning any of these possibilities sends a little chill up your spine, and you probably know why: because Superman doesn't do things like that. In fact, I've rarely been as emotionally disturbed by a comic as when I read the *JSA: Unholy Three* story written by Dan Jolley and Tony Harris when "Superman" (actually the Kryptonian villain Zod in the blue costume) unleashes his powers in lethal fashion. It's kind of like my reaction to any of the comics I've read in which Superman is gone, missing, or, a few years back, dead; something is fundamentally wrong with such a universe. A world without Superman is fundamentally off-center, like the notion of a world without God.

And Superman doesn't kill.

Later in *A Superman for All Seasons*, Luthor has unleashed a deadly virus on Metropolis, and he stands safe again inside his sealed penthouse, while everywhere outside, the virus rages. Superman again floats; he lands; he steps forward. His fist bunched, he first says to Luthor what I'm sure any of us would have thought: "If I were to crash through the glass and drag you out here . . . how long would it be before some Lexcorp employee would appear with the antidote? But . . . I . . . can't take that chance. I can't be like you, Luthor."[14]

For some, this idea of a "self-limiting demigod" doesn't fly. Jeff Jensen, writing in *Entertainment Weekly*, talked of how frustrating it can be—especially in this confusing, terrifying post-9/11 world—not to read stories in which Superman steps up and solves our problems for us, in whatever way that has to happen.[15] But, even given the emotional pitch of the times, I think this misses the point. What makes Superman a vital character is not his power; as we've seen, after he appeared, the world was suddenly densely populated by superheroes who could leap tall buildings in a single bound. But what keeps him vital, as square as he may sometimes seem in comparison to Wolverine, Lobo, Spawn, or Hellboy, is that deep sense of integrity. It is the limitations he places on himself because of his personal morality, taught to him, incidentally, by his human parents. (For Christopher Reeve's Superman, that instruction is also enhanced by the sense of messianic purpose communicated by the data transmissions of his dead Kryptonian father Jor-El [Marlon Brando].) It's the example he gives us that power is only good for so much, the example of superhuman . . . restraint.

And frankly, that's a pretty radical idea in a world where our first response is not to turn the other cheek but to raise the other fist. But an important idea. Gandhi used to say, "An eye for an eye leaves everyone blind." Martin Luther King Jr. preached, "Darkness cannot drive out darkness; only light can do that."[16] Sam Keen points out, "The true revolution in human affairs can never come by armed violence."[17] And the Buddhist nun Pema Chodron says, "The way to stop war is to stop hating the enemy."[18]

OK. Those are nice words. Stop hating. I'm all for that. But there are bad people out there—in the world, in the nation, maybe even in your neighborhood. How on earth can anyone actually live by these sentiments? Bad guys must be met by superior, lethal force.

But I think about Superman, with the power to shatter sky-scrapers, standing outside Luthor's window (or condemning Wonder Woman, one of his closest friends, for choosing to kill an enemy); I think of Scott Summers engaging the evil ideas of a demagogue in "God Loves, Man Kills" instead of splattering his brains with an optic blast; I think of the Israeli pilot Sholem dropping leaflets instead of high explosives.

And I look at our world. Let's take, for example, South Africa, where until the late twentieth-century laws and brutal force kept black human beings at the mercy of white ones. Their spiritual leader, Archbishop Desmond Tutu, spoke for decades to huge crowds, encouraging nonviolent protest. Their political leader, Nelson Mandela, emerged from twenty-seven years in a tiny cell, and he called not for revenge, but for rec-onciliation. And today, South Africa stands as a beacon of hope and achievement in Africa. Those who were hurt have linked justice with forgiveness; they have seen their abusers as mortals like themselves and tried to love them.

And I think of Jesus. In the Gospel narratives, we are con-stantly reminded that, like Superman, Jesus has reserves of power he can call on. When he is tempted by the devil in the Gospel of Luke, Satan urges him to throw himself off a tall tower, reminding him that the Scriptures say, "He has placed you in the care of angels to protect you; they will catch you; you won't so much as stub your toe on a stone."[19] In the

Gospel of Matthew, when one of the disciples (popularly thought to be the hot-headed apostle Peter) draws a sword to try and defend Jesus from the soldiers who have come to arrest him, Jesus turns to him and says, "Put your sword back where it belongs. All who use swords are destroyed by swords. Don't you realize that I am able right now to call to my Father, and twelve companies—more, if I want them—of fighting angels would be here, battle-ready? But if I did that, how would the Scriptures come true that say this is the way it has to be?"[20]

Superhuman restraint. And never more so than in the story of the crucifixion. If Jesus had these powers at his command, why did he remain up on the cross? Man, I wouldn't have; I'd have had those twelve companies of heavily armed angels down double-time to get me down, and then I'd have gotten busy on the bystanders. But that's what we're supposed to learn from the image of Jesus on the cross: the way it has to be. Richard Rohr has said, "Jesus did the victim thing right. He never called for vengeance for his death." Instead he begged God to forgive the people who had put him there to die. It's not surprising, then to hear Rohr argue that Jesus came into the world to solve the essential problem of human hatred.[21] Because Jesus left us an example—the supreme example—of superhuman restraint and revolutionary forgiveness to try to follow.

But, oh, the trying is the hard part. We're not trained for it. Pema Chodron has argued that we ought to establish boot camps for peace in the same way we train soldiers to kill, run perhaps by people like Nelson Mandela, Mother Teresa, and the Dalai Lama:

> Instead of spending hours and hours disciplining ourselves to defeat the enemy, we could spend hours and hours dissolving the causes of war. . . . Such a place might be called boddhisattva training—or training for servants of peace. The word *boddhisattva* refers to those who have committed themselves to the path of compassion.[22]

Thomas Merton seconded this idea of actively learning peace and compassion, noting that mere "pacifism" (a refusal to fight or rejection of war as an ultimate solution) was not enough. We have to be "peacemakers," actively working for justice, not merely passive pacifists:

> The duty of the Christian as a peacemaker is not to be confused with a kind of quietistic inertia that is indifferent to injustice, accepts any kind of disorder, compromises with error and with evil, and gives in to every pressure in order to maintain 'peace at any price.' . . . Peace demands the most heroic labor and the most difficult sacrifice. It demands greater heroism than war.[23]

Merton returned to this last idea again and again in his writing and teaching during the Vietnam War era. Peace is much harder than violence; it requires more discipline, more heroism. So if we are going to save this world, we will have to be superheroes for peace. But how is this to happen?

Well, Pema Chodron's idea of a compassionate boot camp is one example. Beginning on a personal level and extending to the world, we have to learn compassion; we have to learn to love. And we have to work hard at it, because it doesn't come naturally. Jesus tells us in the Gospel of Matthew that we have to love our enemies, pray for those who hate us. "Let them bring out the best in you, not the worst. . . . If all you do is love the lovable, do you expect a bonus? Anybody can do that. If you simply say hello to those who greet you, do you expect a medal?"[24]

So what awaits us in this battle for compassion is a task that's hard for us to do, perhaps one deserving of a medal: We have to, as Bill Jemas wrote in *411*, see even our enemies— maybe *especially* our enemies—as human beings.

Martin Luther King Jr. reminds us that the evil deeds of those who injure us are not the totality of who they are, and he called for us to practice *agape*, the sort of love Christians are supposed to exemplify, "understanding and creative, redemptive goodwill for all men. . . . We love every man because God loves him."[25] Likewise, Sam Keen has written how compassion takes us from a distance—where we see ourselves as opposed to or somehow different from those who might wish us harm—to comprehension and connection: "Compassion destroys our safe observatory and submerges us in the community of the wounded and the mortal."[26]

You can hate a stranger; it is much harder to hate a fellow sufferer. As Abraham Lincoln said once in response to a Northern woman who upbraided him for speaking with compassion about the rebellious South, "Madame, do I not destroy my enemies when I make them my friends?"

The second part of this heroic task of peacemaking is not an effort of compassion and love, but one of faith, and this may in fact be the more challenging effort. It's a challenge that calls us to be people of faith, because if you don't believe in some kind of benevolent God who has some sort of plan for creation, it's almost impossible to imagine that things will ever turn out well. The day-to-day evidence just doesn't support it.

So at the end of things, we come back to eschatology, the study of the end of things. Although everyday events often don't bear it out, people of faith believe that God brought the universe into being for a reason, to gather people to himself, and it is moving through dips and hollows toward some ultimate hope.

In comics, the characters we love face death and destruction month after month, year after year. Evil looms, disaster threatens. But somehow—through willpower or intelligence or supernatural intervention—the tide turns. Martin Luther King Jr. wrote that human history looks just like this: "History is the story of evil forces that advance with seemingly irresistible power only to be crushed by the battering rams of the force of justice."[27]

So to people of faith, the march of history is leading toward a good end, even if this present darkness looks awfully frightening. If we find ourselves up on the cross, most of us are not thinking God is going to put things right in the end; we're thinking *this hurts*, and sending for those well-armed angels. And that's what makes violence such a quickly chosen—and ultimately powerless solution: Strength and power can defeat armies; but as we've seen in Vietnam and Iraq alike, they can't subdue people. And violence can shock and awe someone, but it will never change an opinion, right a wrong, or save a soul.

To pretend otherwise is to sink back into the quagmire that leaves everyone blind. "War is not the answer," Marvin Gaye sang three decades ago. "Only love can conquer hate." And the dude was right.

I once heard pastor and activist Jim Wallis describe world terrorism as being like a swamp filled with mosquitoes. We can go around all day swatting mosquitoes; we can slap them so hard we knock ourselves silly. But we'll never be rid of them until we drain the swamp. What we're talking about in this chapter—love, revolutionary forgiveness, ultimate justice—is how we go about draining the swamp so that some fine day fear, hatred, distrust, and injustice will have dried up.

It's the biggest task there is; by comparison, as Merton noted, lobbing some missiles at somebody is child's play. But this is what life on earth ultimately comes down to: What kind of heroes are we going to be?

When we read comics month after month, go to movies featuring Spider-Man, Batman, the X-Men, the Fantastic Four, it's only partly to see the fight scenes and special effects. We also go because we believe—in some way we may not even consciously acknowledge—in the moral and dramatic fitness of the stories. The characters we love represent something different from the characters who oppose them. There is good and there is evil, and we want to see how good will ultimately triumph.

Always that triumph takes effort, and sometimes we know that it takes sacrifice. When Jean Grey is lost saving those she loves at the end of *X-2*, or when Superman overcomes incredible suffering and seeming death in *Superman Returns* to save the day, we can see a clear analogue to Christ's sacrifice, loving, willing, chosen for a reason.

If we live in a universe ordered by a good God, then suffering, effort, pain, and sacrifice are all leading us ultimately toward redemption.

The radical black activist H. Rap Brown once said, "Violence is as American as cherry pie." And doesn't that seem to be the truth? But I look for a day when "Truth, justice, and the American way" means real peace and justice for everyone, not just the biggest armed response to aggression. I long for a day when instead of giving $10 billion a year to aid the world's starving nations and spending $400 billion on our own defense, we begin to turn those numbers around. I hope for a day when instead of trying to turn our nation into a inviolate island with a missile defense plan, we learn to again see and hear and love the rest of the world enough to make a difference with something besides our fists.

We love the dramatic conflict of violence in our movies and comics. But is that really the way we want to live our lives?

We have heroes who have shown us a better way: Superman, Spider-Man, Captain America.

Martin Luther King Jr., Gandhi, Desmond Tutu.

Jesus of Nazareth.

We've seen from their example what we're meant to be doing here.

Now we have to be heroes, too.

Conclusion

Remember back in the beginning of things, when I talked about our doing something called philosophical reading, looking at comics and movies to see what they could teach us about our own lives and the decisions we make? Now it's time to sum up, and to take those lessons out into a world that desperately needs them.

Lesson One: We need heroes; we believe in saviors.

Throughout human history, as Joseph Campbell showed us, cultures have told stories of heroes who brought hope, solved problems, created meaning. Heroes can be in stories we create, like Superman and Spider-Man, or they can be real. As comics pointed out after 9/11, our real-life heroes—firefighters, police officers, soldiers, emergency medical techs—are every bit as inspiring as those heroes we make up. Maybe more so. But we look to our heroes—whether real, literary, or heroes of faith—to show us how to live, how to ultimately be heroes ourselves.

Lesson Two: We believe evil exists. And while it sometimes appeals to us, we understand that it needs to be conquered.

Some of our favorite comics characters—the Joker, the Red Skull, Magneto, Lex Luthor—are people we wouldn't hang with in everyday life. Their anarchy and power exerts an attraction, but ultimately we side with the good guys. We believe that what the world needs now is—if not love—at least to diminish the suffering and injustice we see all around us. If we didn't believe that, deep down, these stories of good winning out over evil wouldn't be flickering on every multiplex in the land.

Lesson Three: We all have a responsibility to take action to make things better.

Superhero comics depict momentous battles, but Superman doesn't take over the world in an attempt to fix it, and the X-Men don't move into the Oval Office at the end of *X-2*. People of faith believe in a higher power, but most of us believe it's a mistake to think that those powers are going to shape things without any work on our part. As issues of various Superman comics suggest, Superman's example of justice and compassion leading others to work in the world may be a more important legacy than all the times he saved the planet, and so it is with us. Jews must act with justice; Muslims must submit to the leadings of God in their everyday lives; Buddhists must exercise compassion as Buddha taught; Christians must be the healing hands of Christ in the world.

Comics get a lot of things wrong. All men aren't built like Mr. Universe, all women like pinup models. Most people look just plain ridiculous in skintight leotards. If someone punches you in the head, it hurts. Both of you. And so on.

But this they get right, and fortunately, it's the important stuff: we look for heroes as examples of how we're supposed to live, and we can take that example into the ongoing struggle to redeem this world. Maybe we can't, as we said earlier, fly, bend bars, change the course of mighty rivers.

But we can change ourselves: we can become people of peace, love, and compassion. We can do what is right instead of what is expedient. We can question the way things have always been done. We can vote and donate, clean up, give away, speak out, act up. We can try to make a community, a nation, a world we can be proud of.

It'll take bravery. It'll take wisdom. It'll take all the qualities old Shazam handed out to Captain Marvel. And most of us don't have a cape hanging in the closet.

But since when do heroes turn back from a battle worth joining?

I'll see you on the front lines.

Appendix

Essential Graphic Novels and Collections

In this section, I'm recommending twenty-five major works, leaning particularly toward those that grapple with the spiritual themes we've considered in this book. Here you'll find a description and an accounting of some of the points of interest, and an indication of the themes that the books deal with in one way or another. This is only a starting point, of course, but if you're coming to comics fresh, this will start you on the right path and lead you on to other works of merit.

9/11: Artists Respond. Volume One

The best stories in this collection are as good as sequential art gets: powerful, idiosyncratic, art-full. Doug TenNapel's "Pop Grief" shows us how we find grace in unsuspected places; JP Leon's "The Patriot" depicts a person questioning the popular wartime sentiments following 9/11; Mike Carey's script for "In the House of Life" preaches love and family as ways to make sense of a world filled with grief; and Alan Moore and Melinda Gebbie manage in the six pages of "This Is Information" to simultaneously address the subjects of war, terrorism, and reprisal and bring tears to our eyes. Some of these stories are too sentimental; some are too uncritically jingoistic. It was hard to avoid those temptations in the days just after the attacks. But this and similar collections show a side of comics that those who know only superheroes need to experience. Major themes: heroism, justice, power, saviors, the Apocalypse, the Beast, evil, vigilantes, the American way, nonviolence. See also: *9–11: Volume II*, and *Heroes*.

The Authority: Relentless

This collection depicts the launch of one of the most important superhero titles of recent years. It's not a book for kids: *The Authority* not only includes graphic violence and some sexuality, but it also questions authority, particularly comics' traditional adherence to the status quo, "putting the flag back on top of the White House," as a character here puts it. In Warren Ellis's world (beautifully drawn and inked by Bryan Hitch and Paul Neary, beautifully colored by Laura Depuy), saving that world is a radical notion that only begins with solving the immediate looming disaster. There has to be a higher authority, and these folks are it. Major themes: heroism, justice, power, saviors, the Apocalypse, the Beast, evil, vigilantes, the American way. See also: *The Authority: Under New Management*.

Avenger Legends, Vol. 1: Avengers Forever

What would happen if you took superheroes from a number of different time frames and gave them a mission to save all existence? Kurt Busiek's story is an epic that also zeroes in on the characterization of flawed heroes, and Spanish superstar artist Carlos Pacheco illustrates this cosmic story with flair. Major themes: heroism, justice, power, saviors, the Apocalypse, the Beast, evil, the American way.

Batman: The Dark Knight

Dark and disturbing and powerful, this graphic novel reimagines the Batman as a creature of ultimate justice. The art is sometimes shockingly unrealistic, but Frank Miller's moody Expressionism works, somehow. The gritty look and complicated heroism of this book influenced Tim Burton's *Batman* and has influenced superhero comics ever since. Major themes: heroism, justice, power, saviors, the Apocalypse, the Beast, evil, vigilantes, the American way. Also see: Miller's *The Dark Knight Returns* and *Batman: Year One*, and Jeph Loeb and Tim Sale's Batman graphic novels *The Long Halloween* and *The Killing Joke*.

Batman: The Killing Joke

Alan Moore's slim volume came out in the 1980s as one of the earliest graphic novels. Although it is short, it presents major changes in the DC Universe (the Joker shoots and paralyzes Barbara Gordon, the former Batgirl, while the origin of the Joker presented here is the most psychologically complete of any ever offered) as well as creating a powerful tale of where evil comes from. Moore's take on the issue is more sociological and psychological than most, and he presents Batman and the Joker as mirror images, more alike than we had ever imagined. Whether you agree or not, you'll find the book provocative, as all of Moore's best work is. Major themes: heroism, justice, power, saviors, the Beast, evil, vigilantes. See also: Moore's Superman story line *Whatever Happened to the Man of Tomorrow?* for another of his trademark revisions of classic superheroes, and the non-Moore graphic novels *Batman: Absolution* and *Batman: The Chalice*, for other examples of how Batman's psychological complexity makes it possible to examine powerful themes.

Captain America: The New Deal

This relaunch of the venerable *Captain America* title begins in the rubble of 9/11. John Ney Rieber and artist John Cassaday create a Captain America who remains relevant; he's not just an icon of unthinking patriotism, as some writers have made him, but an actual embodiment of everything America stands for— the whole truth/justice/compassion/courage thing. This book examines terrorism from all sides, which may make some readers uncomfortable, but it's important for us to understand why terror seems like a viable solution to some people. Major themes: heroism, justice, power, saviors, the Apocalypse, the Beast, evil, vigilantes, the American way, nonviolence. See also: Ed Brubaker's *Winter Soldier* and *Red Menace*.

Daredevil Visionaries: Kevin Smith

This collection of the first eight stories in the relaunch of Marvel's *Daredevil* superhero title feature the word-heavy scripts of word-heavy indie filmmaker Kevin Smith; fortunately, they're good words, about family, love, loss, faith, and how we do the Father's work in a messed-up world. These issues strongly influenced the movie *Daredevil*. A Christian writer here writes a uniquely Christian hero; Brian Michael Bendis later writes an equally compelling but very different Daredevil. Joe Quesada and Jimmy Palmiotti manage not only to fit in all of Smith's words, but to make them part of stylish and dynamic art. Major themes: heroism, justice, power, saviors, the Apocalypse, the Beast, evil, vigilantes. Also see: Jeph Loeb and Tim Sale's *Daredevil: Yellow*, and Bendis and Alex Maleev's *Daredevil: Decalogue*, which uses the frame of the Ten Commandments to tell a powerful moral tale.

Fables: March of the Wooden Soldiers

In Bill Willingham's Vertigo Comics title where storybook characters actually exist (think of it as *Shrek* for grown-ups), characters battle an evil adversary and their own worst natures to live, love, and work together. It's an inspiring story of the power of love (Snow White and Bigby Wolf—formerly the Big Bad Wolf—are an item) and tolerance (little pigs, storybook animals, giants, and all sorts of other creatures living in comparative harmony), beautifully written and illustrated, with vibrant takes on some of our best-loved characters. The winner (as of this writing) of seven Eisner Awards, the industry's greatest honor, this is one of the best comics currently being published. Major themes:

heroism, justice, power, saviors, the Apocalypse, the Beast, evil. See also: *Storybook Love, The Mean Seasons, Wolves.*

From Hell

A comic (or any work of art) can examine spiritual questions and at the same time be dark, disturbing, and violent; this work examining the crimes of (and theories behind) Jack the Ripper certainly is. Alan Moore spins a grand tale of conspiracy, magic, murder, power, and the coming of the twentieth century. This one may keep you up nights—Eddie Campbell's art is simple, often stylized, but the crimes of the Ripper are gory beyond our remembering, and Moore's characters are at the same time capable of great humanity and great evil. The source of the Johnny Depp film. Major themes: heroism, justice, power, the Apocalypse, the Beast, evil.

Hellblazer: Dangerous Habits

One of the sources for the Keanu Reeves film *Constantine*, this is a good jumping-on point for stories of the rake and magician John Constantine. One point—Constantine is not a nice guy—an apt literary term to pull in here would be "anti-hero"—but he sometimes serves the greater good and pulls the world's fat out of the fire. And sometimes he selfishly or foolishly dooms his friends. Here's a character as important for what he teaches us not to do as what he models; sometimes you love him, and sometimes he saddens you beyond belief. *Hellblazer* takes personified evil very seriously—demons, devils, and the Big D Devil himself are major characters in various stories. Major themes: heroism, justice, power, saviors, the Apocalypse, the Beast, evil. Also see: *Son of Man, Setting Sun, Haunted, Stations of the Cross.*

Hellboy: Wake the Devil

Mike Mignola's paranormal investigator Hellboy was the product of the pairing of a witch and a demon—maybe a demon prince!—but he shows that one can choose good (like Superman, Hellboy had a human adoptive father) instead of one's evil nature. In story after story, Hellboy faces supernatural evil head-on—or perhaps hand-on—and the title is never as good as when Mignola illustrates his own stories, as he does here. Major themes: heroism, justice, power, saviors, the Apocalypse, the Beast, evil, vigilantes, the American way, nonviolence. See also: *The Chained Coffin*, *The Right Hand of Doom*, *Conqueror Worm*, and the Mignola-scribed Bureau of Paranormal Defense (BPRD) titles.

Kingdom Come

Rarely do mainstream comics so clearly use and acknowledge faith and religious traditions as this book by Mark Waid and Alex Ross. But the main character, a minister, was modeled after (and by) Ross's father, himself a minister; another main character is the Spectre, God's own superhero. So in this tale of the end of the world, Scripture and superheroes commingle. Ross's paintings are visually stunning, and the story line takes mainstream superheroes where they've never gone while simultaneously reaffirming some of our deepest beliefs. Major themes: heroism, justice, power, saviors, the Apocalypse, the Beast, evil, vigilantes, the American way, nonviolence. See also: *Justice League of America: The Nail*, a story of how some things are just destined to be; *JLA/JSA: Virtue and Vice*, a story about how we can be taken over by sins; and Darwyn Cooke's *The New Frontier*, a stylish and moving story about the world's greatest heroes.

Maus: A Survivor's Tale (Part 1): My Father Bleeds History

Underground comics went mainstream with this graphic novel depicting the Holocaust experiences of writer/artist Art Spiegelman's family. The simple trope of drawing the characters as funny animals—the Jews as mice, the Nazis as cats, the Poles as pigs—lets us look at events that often repel us, and learn lessons about fate, memory, and the power of art. Major themes: the Holocaust, power, evil, justice, heroism. See also *Maus II: And Here My Troubles Began.*

Midnight Nation

J. Michael Straczynski creates an epic story that connects the dots from God to Satan to Lazarus to angels to us. Rarely do mainstream comics so effectively blend action and spirituality. Gary Frank's women are stunning and his demons are chilling, while Matt Milla's coloring work here is among the best you'll ever see in comic art. Major themes: heroism, justice, power, saviors, the Apocalypse, the Beast, evil, vigilantes, the American way.

The Mystery Play

This powerful and very literary graphic novel from writer Grant Morrison—best known for his superhero stories—features beautiful painted art from Jon J. Muth. It's a philosophical thriller about a murder—the murder of "God," in fact—committed during the restaging of a medieval mystery play in England, and the mysterious detective who comes to investigate it for his own reasons. Religious images and concepts like redemption and atonement permeate the book. Major themes: justice, power, saviors, the Apocalypse, the Beast, evil.

Planetary: All Over the World, and Other Stories

This collection of the first stories from the Wildstorm (DC) title written by Warren Ellis and drawn by John Cassaday isn't directly interested in spiritual questions, although each issue tends to contain something supernatural. But it is the smartest and most entertaining title in comics today, drawing from popular culture as diverse as the Fantastic Four, Japanese monster movies, Hong Kong action films, and the pulp magazines of the 1930s. A terrific conspiracy/superhero book, this collection will introduce you to a group of "detectives" trying to uncover the secrets of the world and help people in the process.

Themes: heroism, justice, power, saviors, evil. See also: *Planetary: The Fourth Man* and *Planetary/Batman: Night on Earth*.

Powers: Who Killed Retro Girl?

Brian Michael Bendis's stock-in-trade is the crime story, and that's what he returns to over and over in his early graphic novels, in *Daredevil*, and in this quirky, funny, and genuinely moving series about cops trying to bring justice to a world full of superpowered heroes, villains, and folks who straddle that line. Lead character Detective Christian Walker (could this name be a tiny bit symbolic?) is a contemporary Superman—moral, courageous, just—and he and his partner, Deena Pilgrim (symbolism, anyone?) investigate crimes that involve "powers," like this murder of an iconic superheroine. Stylish layouts from Michael Avon Oeming make Bendis's talky scripts visually interesting. Major themes: heroism, justice, power, saviors, the Beast, evil, vigilantes. Also see: *Powers: Roleplay* and *Powers: Little Deaths*.

Road to Perdition

A visually beautiful and spiritually complex tale of gangsters during Prohibition, and the basis for the film starring Tom Hanks and Paul Newman. Crime writer Max Allan Collins creates a deadly mob enforcer who is also a family man and devout Catholic. How all those things balance—or don't balance—also raises questions about how we rationalize violence in the world, particularly as a solution in wartime. Themes: heroism, justice, power, the Beast, evil, vigilantes, the American way, nonviolence.

Sandman: Season of Mists

Some folks have called the ongoing stories featuring Neil Gaiman's character Sandman/Dream the greatest comics ever, and in this fourth collected volume, the stories really began to hit their stride. Dream interacts with his extended family "The Endless" (Death, Destiny, Despair, et al.), wrestles with Lucifer, and goes to hell. Just an average day in the life of this cosmic title. New editions, recolored to fix one of the few flaws of these stories (as in *Watchmen*, the color separations are archaic), are coming out. Major themes: heroism, justice, power, evil. See also: *The Kindly Ones* and *Endless Nights*.

A Superman for All Seasons

Jeph Loeb and Tim Sale remember the "man" in Superman, who has often been ignored by storytellers over the decades. Here we're reminded of the simpler time and place that Superman came from and how desperately we still need those "all-American" values. These pages remind us of Norman Rockwell paintings and John Ford westerns; they also make us believe a man can fly. Traditional and deeply inspirational: for my money, the best Superman ever. Major themes: heroism, justice, power, saviors, evil, the American way, nonviolence. See also: Loeb and Sale's *Daredevil: Yellow* (already mentioned); other terrific "retro" titles include *Spider-Man: Blue*, *Batman: Haunted Knight*, and *Batman: Dark Victory*.

The Ultimates: Homeland Security

Mark Millar's ultratopical retake on the Avengers privileges ambiguity and foregrounds the question of what happens when all-too-human heroes are empowered to act on our behalf. In later story lines, the Ultimates will be deployed as weapons of mass destruction overseas—and Millar will tie America's military and economic policies directly to the terrorism that plagues us today. This superhero title is not for kids or the easily offended. Major themes: heroism, justice, power, saviors, the Apocalypse, the Beast, evil, vigilantes, the American way, nonviolence. See also: *Gods and Monsters*.

Ultimate Spider-Man Vol. 1: Power and Responsibility

When Marvel relaunched some of its most popular series as new "ultimate" versions a few years ago, it freed them from the fifty years of history (in comics, called "continuity") that most new/young readers don't know or could care less about. These "first" Spider-Man stories closely conform to the character's classic origin, but updated by Brian Michael Bendis's fine ear for contemporary dialogue, the series comes to life in the same way it must have originally for kids in the 1960s. In these pages, Peter Parker/Spider-Man learns the lesson that will drive his life: being a hero is about being responsible to and for others. Major themes: heroism, justice, power, saviors, the Beast, evil, vigilantes, the American way, nonviolence.

Watchmen

Alan Moore's graphic novel about a world without superheroes takes a close look at the narrative conventions of comics and asks hard questions about violence, justice, power, and godhood. While Dave Gibbons's art seems somewhat dated, partly because of the primary-colors coloring, the story remains relevant and moving, as its characters live, love, and seek to do the right thing in a world much more complex than that of traditional comics. *Watchmen* and Frank Miller's *The Dark Knight* were the watershed comics of the 1980s. Major themes: heroism, justice, power, saviors, the Apocalypse, the Beast, evil, vigilantes, the American way. See also: Moore's take on the police procedural comic in a superhero mythos, *Top Ten*, and his dystopian vision of a world of the future, *V for Vendetta*.

Wolverine

Longtime X-Men scripter Chris Claremont and artist Frank Miller redefined Wolverine and in the process made him into one of the most popular comics characters ever. Their process was simple: make him more complex. Instead of just an animal in human form, they made him a person struggling with his violent urges, a person with regrets and aspirations, a person with a soul. Ninjas, samurai, Zen, love, and one bad superhero. Major themes: heroism, justice, power, the Beast, evil. See also:

Barry Windsor-Smith's *Weapon X*, an account of Wolverine's indoctrination and conversion into a living weapon.

X-Men: God Loves, Man Kills

Chris Claremont wrote what many consider the definitive X-Men book with this early graphic novel (1982!) about prejudice, violence, and religion. The basis for the movie *X-2*, Claremont's script seems a little talky in comparison to most of today's superhero titles, but it has otherwise held up well, and its message of peace and tolerance is just as necessary today as when it was first presented. Major themes: heroism, justice, power, saviors, the Apocalypse, the Beast, evil, vigilantes, the American way, nonviolence. Also see: Claremont and John Byrne's *Dark Phoenix Saga* and *X-Men: Days of Future Past*.

Notes

Preface

1. Karen Armstrong, *The Battle for God: A History of Fundamentalism* (New York: Ballantine Books, 2001), xv.

Introduction

1. Karl Kesel, *Fantastic Four* 3.56 (2002): 26.

2. Ibid., 28–30.

3. Paul Johnson, *A History of the Jews* (New York: Perennial, 1987), 265.

4. Jeffrey Weiss, "Comic Faith: The Thing's Religion Revealed," *Dallas Morning News*, August 24, 2002, http://www.beliefnet.com/story/113/story_11303_1.html.

5. Jeffrey Overstreet, "Looking Closer's 30 Favorite Films of 2003," *Looking Closer*, http://lookingcloser.org/awards/Awards-2003.htm.

6. Ron Grover, "*300*'s Lessons for Hollywood," *Business Week*, April 9, 2007, http://www.businessweek.com/bwdaily/dnflash/content/apr2007/db20070409_889613.htm?chan=top+news_top+news+index.

7. *Wizard* 187 (2007): 15.

8. "Superhero Marquees," *San Jose Mercury*, Feb. 9, 2003, 3E.

9. Roberta E. Pearson and William Uricchio, "Notes from the Batcave," in *The Many Lives of the Batman: Critical Approaches to a Superhero and his Media*, ed. Pearson and Uricchio (London: Routledge, 1991), 10.

10. John Shelton Lewis and Robert Jewett, *The Myth of the American Superhero* (Grand Rapids: Eerdmans, 2002), 6.

11. Lewis and Jewett, *Myth of the American Superhero*, 6–7.

Modern Heroes

1. "Sam Raimi's Heroes," *Screentalk*, May/June 2002: 41.

2. Joseph Campbell and Bill Moyers, *The Power of Myth* (New York: Anchor Books, 1988), 166.

3. Burton Mack, *Who Wrote the New Testament?* (New York: HarperSanFrancisco, 1996), 304.

4. Campbell and Moyers, *Power of Myth*, 151.

5. "Sam Raimi's Heroes," 42.

Look, Up in the Sky!

1. "Red Son Rising," *Wizard* 140 (May 2003): 131.

2. Jules Feiffer, *The Great Comic Book Heroes*, 1965 (New York: Fantagraphics, 2003), 8–9.

3. "How the Jews Created the Comic Book Industry, Part One: The Golden Age (1933–1955)," *Reform Judaism*, http://www.ariekaplan.com/kingscomicspart1.htm.

4. Alan Moore, *Superman: Whatever Happened to the Man of Tomorrow* (New York: DC Comics, 1997), 46.

5. Richard Corliss, "The Gospel of Superman," *Time*, June 18, 2006, http://www.time.com/time/magazine/article/0,9171,1205367,00.html.

6. Chris Seay and Greg Garrett, *The Gospel Reloaded: Exploring Spirituality and Faith in the Matrix* (Colorado Springs, CO: Piñon Press, 2003), 105.

7. *A Superman for All Seasons* (New York: DC Comics, 1999), 189, 195.

8. *The Book of Common Prayer* (New York: Oxford University Press, 1990), 864.

9. Eugene Peterson, *The Message* (Colorado Springs, CO: NavPress, 2002), 1942–43.

10. *Superman vs. Darkseid: Apokolips Now!* (New York: DC Comics, 2003), 1.

11. Ibid., 37–38.

12. Ben Morse, "Superman," *Wizard* 183 (January 2007): 64.

13. Mark Moring, "The 'Savior' Returns," *Christianity Today*, June 26, 2006, http://www.christianitytoday.com/movies/interviews/bryansinger.html.

With Great Power Comes Great Responsibility

1. Stan Lee, "Introduction," *Marvel Masterworks: The Amazing Spiderman* (New York: Marvel, 2003), i.

2. *Marvel Masterworks*, 10.

3. Ibid., 13.

4. Eugene Peterson, *The Message* (Colorado Springs, CO: NavPress, 2002), 1679.

5. Thomas Merton, *No Man Is an Island* (New York: Harvest, 1978), 10.

6. Peterson, *Message*, 1797.

7. Desmond Tutu, *The Rainbow People of God* (New York: Doubleday, 1994), 158.

8. Martin Luther King Jr., "Our God Is Able," in *Strength to Love* (Philadelphia: Fortress Press, 1963), 107.

Truth, Justice, and the American Way

1. Cormac McCarthy, *All the Pretty Horses* (New York: Knopf, 1992), 168.

2. Martin Luther King Jr., "A Tough Mind and a Tender Heart," in *Strength to Love* (Philadelphia: Fortress Press, 1963), 10.

3. Bryan Magee, *The Story of Thought: The Essential Guide to the History of Western Philosophy* (London: Dorling Kindersley Books, 1998), 189.

4. Chris Seay and Greg Garrett, *The Gospel Reloaded* (Colorado Springs, CO: Piñon Press, 2003), 25.

5. Karen Armstrong, *The Battle for God* (New York: Ballantine Books, 2000), xiii.

6. Charles Kimball, *When Religion Becomes Evil: Five Warning Signs* (New York: HarperSanFrancisco, 2002), passim.

7. Christopher Sharrett, "Batman and the Twilight of the Idols: An Interview with Frank Miller," in *The Many Lives of the Batman: Critical Approaches to a Superhero and His Media*, ed. Roberta Pearson and William Uricchio (London: Routledge, 1991), 36.

8. *Batman: Absolution* (New York: DC Comics, 2002), 11.

9. Ibid., 47.

10. John Ziesler, *The Oxford Companion to the Bible* (New York: Oxford University Press, 1993), s.v. "Righteousness."

11. Joseph Telushkin, *Biblical Literacy* (New York: William Morrow, 1997), 327.

12. Les Daniels, *DC Comics: Sixty Years of the World's Favorite Comic Book Heroes* (New York: Bulfinch, 1995), 22.

13. Desmond Tutu, "We Drink Water to Fill Our Stomachs," in *The Rainbow People of God* (New York: Doubleday, 1994), 37.

14. Robert Jewett and John Shelton Lawrence, *Captain America and the Crusade against Evil: The Dilemma of Zealous Nationalism* (Grand Rapids: Eerdmans, 2003), 42–43.

15. Forrest Church, *The American Creed* (New York: St. Martin's, 2002), xiii.

16. *Captain America* 4.11 (2003): 21–22.

17. "Talk of the Nation," National Public Radio, May 2, 2006, http://www.npr.org/templates/story/story.php?storyId=5376903.

18. Ben Morse, "Captain America," *Wizard* 187 (May 2007): 34.

19. *Fantastic Four* 540 (2006): n.p.

20. Gen. 22:1–10 NRSV.

21. Bruce Feiler, *Abraham: A Journey to the Heart of Three Faiths* (New York: Perennial, 2004), 99.

22. "Conservative" here is not a political label, but a cultural or perhaps even an intellectual one: it designates a mind-set that the "way we have always done things" should remain our default setting.

23. Frank Miller, *The Dark Knight Returns* (New York: DC Comics, 1986), 119.

24. Ibid., 190.

25. Robert F. Kennedy, *Make Gentle the Life of this World: The Vision of Robert F. Kennedy*, ed. Maxwell Taylor Kennedy (New York: Broadway Books, 1999), 27.

The Problem of Evil

1. *Batman: Year One* (New York: DC Comics, 1988), 2.

2. *Planetary/Batman: Night on Earth* (New York: DC Comics, 2003), 2.

3. Samuel A. Meier, *The Oxford Companion to the Bible* (New York: Oxford University Press, 1993), s.v. "Evil."

4. Peter Gomes, *The Good Book: Reading the Bible with Mind and Heart* (New York: William Morrow, 1996), 217.

5. Ibid., 218–19.

6. Chris Seay and Greg Garrett. *The Gospel Reloaded: Exploring Spirituality and Faith in the Matrix* (Colorado Springs, CO: Piñon Press, 2003), 133.

7. Gomes, *Good Book*, 259–60.

8. Max Allan Collins, *Road to Perdition* (New York: Pocket, 1998), 22.

9. Ibid., 190.

10. Mark Moring, "Spidey Gets Spiritual," *Christianity Today*, May 5, 2007, http://www.christianitytoday.com/movies/interviews/samraimy.html.

11. Thomas Merton, *No Man Is an Island* (New York: Harcourt Brace, 1983), 3.

12. Dalai Lama, *Ethics for the New Millennium* (New York: Riverhead, 1999), 234.

13. Martin Luther King Jr., *I Have a Dream* (New York: HarperCollins, 1992), 92.

14. Augustine, *Confessions* VII.xii (18), trans. Henry Chadwick (Oxford: Oxford University Press, 1991), 125.

15. Bryan Magee, *The Story of Thought* (London: DK Publishing, 1998), 174.

16. *The Fantastic Four: The Trial of Galactus* (New York: Marvel Comics, 1989), n.p.

17. Ibid.

Vigilante Justice

1. *The Oxford Essential Dictionary of the U.S. Military*, http://www.oxfordreference.com/views/ENTRY.html?subview=Main&entry=t63.e8869.

2. "A Sketch *of the* Causes, Operations *and* Results *of the* San Francisco Vigilance Committee in 1856," 1874, http://www.books-about-california.com/Pages/Sketchs_Vigiliance_Committee/Vigilance_Committee_text.html.

3. John Shelton Lawrence and Robert Jewett, *The Myth of the American Superhero* (Grand Rapids: Eerdmans, 2002), 40.

4. Joe Klein, *The Natural* (New York: Doubleday, 2002), 72

5. Lawrence and Jewett, *Myth of the American Superhero*, 40.

6. "Standards of the Comic Code Authority," http://www.comics.dm.net/codetext.htm.

7. Joseph Telushkin, *Biblical Literacy* (New York: William Morrow, 1997), 446.

8. *Wizard* 145 (2003): 52.

9. *Superman/Batman* 1 (2003): 7.

10. *The Nail* (New York: DC Comics, 1998), 20.

11. *Batman* 614 (2003): 31.

12. *Watchmen* (New York: DC Comics, 1987), 27.

13. *Daredevil* 2.45 (2003): 8.

14. *Daredevil* 2.44 (2003): 20, 22.

15. Martin Luther King Jr., "A Tough Mind and a Tender Heart," in *Strength to Love* (Philadelphia: Fortress Press, 1963), 14,

16. Eugene Peterson, *The Message* (Colorado Springs, CO: NavPress, 2002), 1651.

The Beast

1. Anthony Stevens, "The Shadow in History and Literature," in *Meeting the Shadow*, ed. Jeremiah Abrams and Connie Zweig (New York: Putnam's, 1991), 28.

2. Eugene Peterson, *The Message* (Colorado Springs, CO: NavPress, 2002), 1947.

3. Rollo May, *Love and Will* (New York: Norton, 1969), 121, 129.

4. *Midnight Nation* (Orange, CA: Image Comics, 2003), n.p.

5. Jeff Jensen, "Green Thumbing," in *Entertainment Weekly* (Summer Double Issue 2003): 144.

6. Ibid., "Mad World," in *Entertainment Weekly*, http://www.ew.com/ew/report/0,6115,454781_1||455601|0_0_,00.html.

7. Peter Sanderson, *Ultimate X-Men* (New York: DK Publishing, 2003), 64.

8. *God Loves, Man Kills—Special Edition* (New York: Marvel, 2003), n.p.

9. *Wolverine* (New York: Marvel, 1990), n.p.

10. Ibid.

11. *Mythology: The DC Comics Art of Alex Ross* (New York: Pantheon Books, 2003), n.p.

12. Peterson, *Message*, 2044.

13. *JLA/Spectre: Soul War #1* (New York: DC Comics, 2003), 8–11.

14. *JLA/Spectre: Soul War #2* (New York: DC Comics, 2003), 46.

15. *Wolverine*.

16. Ps. 130: 1 (NRSV).

The Apocalypse

1. Lee Quinby, *Millennial Seduction: A Skeptic Confronts Apocalyptic Culture* (Ithaca, NY: Cornell University Press, 1999), 5.

2. Mircea Eliade, *Myths, Dreams, and Mysteries*, trans. Phillip Mairet (New York: Harper & Row, 1961), 243.

3. David S. Dockery, "On (Mis)Reading the 'Signs of the Times,'" *Academic Forum*, http://www.uu.edu/centers/christld/academicforum/faculty/article.cfm?ID=11.

4. *Watchmen*, chap. 1 (New York: DC Comics, 1987), 1, 24.

5. Ibid., chap. 12, 20.

6. Ibid.

7. Ibid., 18.

8. Ibid., 27.

9. *Mythology: The DC Comics Art of Alex Ross* (New York: Pantheon Books, 2003), n.p.

10. *Kingdom Come* (New York: DC Comics, 1997), 44.

11. Ibid., 49.

12. Ibid., 215.

13. Ibid., 163.

14. Val J. Sauer Jr., *The Eschatology Handbook* (Atlanta: John Knox Press, 1981), vii–ix.

15. Lee Quinby, *Millennial Seduction: A Skeptic Confronts Apocalyptic Culture* (Ithaca, NY: Cornell University Press, 1999), 3.

16. *Kingdom Come*, 203.

17. John Polkinghorne, *The God of Hope and the End of the World* (New Haven, CT: Yale University Press, 2002), 47–48.

The Holocaust

1. Don Markstein's Toonopedia, "Maus," http://www.toonopedia.com/maus.htm.

2. Art Spiegelman, *Maus: A Survivor's Tale* (New York: Pantheon, 1986), 23.

3. Ibid., 157.

4. Eugene Peterson, *The Message* (Colorado Springs, CO: NavPress, 2002), 36.

5. *X-Men: God Loves, Man Kills—Special Edition* (New York: Marvel, 2003), n.p.

6. *Weapon X* 5 (March 2003): 23.

7. Thomas Merton, "Auschwitz: A Family Camp," in *The Nonviolent Alternative* (New York: Farrar, Straus & Giroux, 1980), 159.

8. *X-Men: Days of Future Past* (New York: Marvel, 2000), 23.

9. *X-Men: God Loves, Man Kills*, 1–3.

10. *Wizard: X-Men Special*, 2003: 9.

11. *X-Men: God Loves, Man Kills*, n.p.

12. Ibid.

13. Ibid.

The End of Violence

1. *Captain America Vol. 1: The New Deal* (New York: Marvel, 2003), n.p.

2. Ibid.

3. Ibid.

4. *9-11: Artists Respond*, vol. 1 (Milwaukie, OR: Dark Horse, 2002), 167.

5. Marc Ellis, "On Revolutionary Forgiveness," in *Revolutionary Forgiveness* (Waco, TX: Baylor University Press, 2000), 275–76.

6. *4-11* 1 (2003): n.p.

7. Ibid.

8. Richard Rohr, "Little Fears, Little Enemies" (lecture, Episcopal Theological Seminary of the Southwest, Austin, TX, Feb. 9, 2004).

9. Cormac McCarthy, *Cities of the Plain* (New York: Knopf, 1998), 191.

10. *Amazing Spider-Man Vol. 2: Revelations* (New York: Marvel, 2002), n.p.

11. *9-11: Artists Respond*, 185–90.

12. *9-11: Artists Respond*. vol. 2 (New York: DC, 2002), 122.

13. *A Superman for All Seasons* (New York: DC Comics, 1999), 120–22.

14. Ibid., 143–45.

15. Jeff Jensen, "Cape Cowed," *Entertainment Weekly*, Summer Movie Double Issue, 2003, 156.

16. Martin Luther King Jr., *Strength to Love* (Philadelphia: Fortress Press, 1963), 51.

17. Sam Keen, *To Love and Be Loved* (New York: Bantam, 1997), 98.

18. Pema Chodron, *When Things Fall Apart* (Boston: Shambhala, 1997), 111.

19. Eugene Peterson, *The Message* (Colorado Springs, CO: NavPress, 2002), 1858.

20. Ibid., 1801.

21. Rohr, "Little Fears, Little Enemies."

22. Chodron, *When Things Fall Apart*, 98.

23. Thomas Merton, "The Christian in World Crisis," in *The Nonviolent Alternative* (New York: Farrar, Straus & Giroux, 1980), 34–35.

24. Peterson, *Message*, 1753.

25. King, *Strength to Love*, 49–51.

26. Keen, *To Love and Be Loved*, 101.

27. King, *Strength to Love*, 109.

About the Author

Greg Garrett's previous books on faith and culture are *The Gospel According to Hollywood*, and *The Gospel Reloaded: Exploring Spirituality and Faith in the Matrix*, which he cowrote with Chris Seay. He is also the author of the novels *Free Bird* (chosen by *Publishers Weekly* and the *Denver Rocky Mountain News* as one of the best first novels of 2002) and *Cycling*, the memoir *Crossing Myself*, and numerous short stories, articles, and essays on film, writing, faith, and politics. Greg is Professor of English at Baylor University, where he has twice won university-wide honors for his teaching, and writer-in-residence at the Episcopal Theological Seminary of the Southwest. His work has been reviewed or covered by major media, including *USA Today*, National Public Radio, Headline News, CBS Radio, *Christianity Today*, and radio stations and newspapers from coast to coast. Greg lives in Austin, Texas, with his sons Jake and Chandler.

CPSIA information can be obtained
at www.ICGtesting.com
Printed in the USA
BVHW080028290819
556879BV00002B/63/P

Praise for the first edition:

"Not just a great book about the spirituality of comic books . . . . one of the most insightful books I have read on any topic in a long time."
—Kevin Miller, hollywoodjesus.com

"Proof that comics can inspire thoughtful and witty reflection on their own terms."
—Edirin Ibru, *Books & Culture*

SPIDER-MAN. BATMAN. THE X-MEN. THE FANTASTIC FOUR. Comic books and the characters they have spawned have become twenty-first-century mythology. Greg Garrett helps us see the profound depth that can be found in the glossy, fast-paced, and often violent world of comics, graphic novels, and the films they inspire.

Holy Superheroes! provides extensive discussions of some of our most beloved comic heroes and concludes with an appendix of twenty-five comics and graphic novels for discussion of spirituality and comics.

GREG GARRETT is the author of several books, including *The Gospel according to Hollywood* and *Crossing Myself: A Story of Spiritual Rebirth.* He is a professor of English at Baylor University.

Religion & Popular Culture
ISBN 978-0-664-23191-0
90000

WJK

9 780664 231910